Canadian Institutions And Children's Best Interests: *Henriflavipeterism* As The Quebec 'Money-Only' Sole Custody Case Meant For The Hall Of Shame?

I0110292

Peter Ateh-Afac Fossungu

Langaa Research & Publishing CIG
Mankon, Bamenda

Publisher:
Langaa RPCIG

Langaa Research & Publishing Common Initiative Group
P.O. Box 902 Mankon
Bamenda
North West Region
Cameroon
Langaagrp@gmail.com
www.langaa-rpcig.net

Distributed in and outside N. America by African Books Collective
orders@africanbookscollective.com
www.africanbookscollective.com

ISBN: 9956-762-25-3

DISCLAIMER
All views expressed in this publication are those of the author and do not
necessarily reflect the views of Langaa RPCIG.

Dedicated To The Millions Of Children Undeservingly Suffering Solely Because Of The Scheming Of So-Called Parents, Fortified By The Complicity Of Canadian Institutions

Table of Contents

v

Introduction

For about four years I have done everything any reasonable and caring person would do to work hand in hand with Flavie for the betterment of us all. But it has been unfruitful because it is very hard to help a nonoselfist or someone who only believes that he or she is entitled to sit around and do nothing other than to be on the phone 24/7 while others do everything for him or her. And, yet it is amazing that such a person gives no bit of respect to those doing those things (Fossungu, 2015a: 32).

This book is centred on *Henriflavipeterism* whose other legal name is *Fossungu v. Bayiha*.[1] I initially thought of reporting here as a third-party but swiftly changed my mind on that. Because (you yourself can bear with me that) much of the authentic force of the narrative would not only get lost in that fashion. But also it is because of the untruthfulness deriving from the knowledge that I would then "be telling you my story without actually letting you know it is my story" (Fossungu, 2013: 1). Personally involved in it as I am, I still think you can comfortably count on my objectivity in reporting it as it is. Not only because of what Rosetta Coding has already recommended to you (see Fossungu, 2015a: xi-xii). But also because, being a well-known *crisebacologist*, "I have learnt to separate things and deal with them accordingly in a balanced or even-handed manner" (Fossungu, 2015a: 32). I hope the experts in the relevant fields can find the material presented herein useful for their further specialized and in-depth analyses. In an earlier work I described some Canadian courts as 'Mechanical Courts' staffed by a Gang of Liars (Fossungu, 2015a: 58-59 & 3). The "controversial" robotized-courts thesis

---

[1] *Peter Ateh-Afac Fossungu v. Henriette-Flavi Bayiha*, Suit N° 500-04-060196-137 of Montreal's Cour Supérieure, Chambre de la Famille.

was posited with particular reference to Ontario's London Family High Court. Now, I want you to meticulously go through another court story in our beloved world-wide Montréal in Quebec[2] and tell me what you think about the charge(s) as also noted in Fossungu (2015b: 192).

On Wednesday April 1, 2015 I was at 4251 Badgley in Montreal, the day-care where my two sons usually spend most of their week days. I was there to hand-deliver a registered mail that I had just received from the day-care owner, Filomena Pina Gonzalez. She got the unopened package, with me explaining to her that I had just taken its delivery from the Post Office that same day only in order to bring it back to her to avoid the waste of time that non-delivery would entail before she would get the returned mail. Since the children were not there that Wednesday morning (11.00 AM), I inquired if they no longer attend the day-care. Filomena's explication was that they still do; but that on that day they were spending the day with their mother who had indicated that she had somewhere to go to with them.

How disappointing! I had gone there especially to also see and be with my boys on the birthday of their brother in London. Yes! It was Nguajong's birthday and yet I couldn't be there in London with him, nor even call him that evening to wish him all the things we all know of. Not that I really didn't want to talk to my first son on his special day. Just to avoid the embarrassing encounters: from the 'money-only' words that their mother usually puts in their mouths on my calling there.[3]

---

2 "Montréal seems to have a special flavour. That explains why it is the one Canadian city I have had to call home for a long, long time. Like most Canadian mega-cities, Montreal has it all. You just do not have to be actually living in any specific country of the world to be there. Live in Montréal and you can rightly boast of having lived the world over. 'I Love My Montréal' is the way we, *les Montréalais*, proudly put it" (Fossungu, 2015a: x-xi).

3 You easily pick up the money-only attitude from Scholastica Achankeng Asahchop's endless 'friendly reminders' on child support. One

I didn't call too on March 2 which is Ngunyi's not just because of the above reason. I was on the Montreal-Windsor-Montreal road all through that day and the next, trying to bring up most of my stuff back to Montreal and also attend the court session three days later. Because no call had been forthcoming in March, I made it a point not to call in April also, particularly to avoid giving the wrong impression of discriminating.

As I never saw the Montreal children, I went back to their day-care on Friday, April 3, to also hand over the day-care cheque for that month. They were there that Friday. But I was not happy at all just seeing them. I cried enormously, both inside and outside. My children are *all* always very excited seeing or hearing from me, of course. If there is one thing I have been blessed with, it is the strong bond that I have with *all* my children, their mothers' bond-destroying schemes notwithstanding. Take Kelie who only recently (in 2010) knew that her father was alive, and then only actually first met and knew me (with that knowledge) in May 2014. With the others, one could say it is because I was always the first they bonded with on tumbling out of the womb. That was not the case with Kelie; but the unbreakable bond is still there and did not manifested itself only on our first meeting and being physically present. On December 10, 2014 she wrote this email to me

---

of Scholastica's reminders came in on Thursday, September 20, 2012 1:19 PM stating that "I am still patiently waiting. S.A" On Thursday, September 27, 2012 at 2.32 PM I replied, saying: "I have not been able to find someone going to town. I'll be going there tomorrow myself to post the cheque which you should be getting any time next week. PAF." And on Friday, June 16, 2012 7:27 PM my 'Cheque Sent Instead' message told Scholastica that "I could not get to town today before the banks closed; so I have instead mailed a cheque of 428.00$, covering the month of May 2012. I will try to see if I could henceforth make the transfer through internet. I am yet to set up the service. Greet Ngunyi and Nguajong for me. Take care and bye now. PAF"

(with subject title "lettre a mon père cherie" [4]) that I would like to share with you to cement the point.

But I just didn't like what I was seeing in the two boys that morning: very poorly dressed, hungry-looking, sad-faced and emotionally-exhausted young boys. I had to immediately revise my weekend plans. That same evening, at about 7.00 PM, I called their mother to request having them for the weekend. Flavie said it was alright, and I indicated that I would be coming for them at 9.30 AM next day and to return them Sunday evening. She then said she would want them back

---

[4] This letter that represents the one singular thing that greatly lifted my spirit at a period I was almost without one read as follows :

Tu sais papa, tu es la seule personne au monde qui me connaisse vraiment, il n'y en a pas dix, il n'y en a pas cent, il n'y en a qu'une et c'est toi...

Tu es le seul qui arrive vraiment à me définir, le seul qui me comprenne en profondeur, qui m'aide à réaliser, à bien réparer. J'ai parfois mal agi papa, mal interagi avec les autres ou même avec toi, mais ta bonté m'a guidé et ta patience m'a prouvé la grande âme que tu es. J'ai pu parfois te décevoir, mais jamais en toi je n'ai senti un manque d'amour infini... Tu as toujours su me faire cadeau d'une seconde chance, quand j'y pense j'ai toujours pu réacquérir ce qu'il y a de plus cher à mes yeux: ta confiance. Tu as su me faire percevoir en profondeur, dans nos nombreuses conversations qui, en laissant défiler les heures, m'ont fait conscientiser mes peurs ou ont tout simplement ouvert davantage mon cœur...

Je ne t'aime pas seulement pour tout ce que tu fais pour moi, papa, je t'aime pour la personne que tu es en ce moment, pour les milliers de vies que tu sauves à chaque instant de la tienne, tout comme la mienne. Je t'aime pour qui tu es réellement, pour ton rayonnement, ta joie éternelle, ton amour inconditionnel.

De la part de ta fille kelly. Je t'aime pour toujours papa [omission dots are original].

My Loose Translation (MLT): *My dear father, do you know that you are the only one who really understands me so well? You are the only person that gives me a real definition of who I truly am; the only that truly loves me for just who I am, including my failings; the singular person who helps numerous other persons, including me, to mature in understanding and progressing in life. In short, daddy, I love you not just because of what you have done and are still doing for me, but mostly because of the type of person that you are — always glowing with joy and with an unfailing and infinite love and concern for the wellbeing of others.*

Saturday evening since they had already been invited "somewhere" on Sunday. Well, I always try to avoid argument and confrontation. I said therefore that I had no problem with that. At 9.30 AM on Saturday I was there to get them, having called before leaving the house. Flavie then insisted on my having them back by 6.30 PM. No surprise at all. The astonishment would come when she would be asking me to bring them at the specified time to a church with address on Chemin de la Côte-Des-Neiges (CDN), saying Peter, Jr. knows the place! Flavie of all people and church! How come? As I said earlier, I like to eschew any confrontation with her in the presence of the children especially. Back at home with the children, I called her, got the full address, and made this clear to her: Whenever I want to have the children and you find it inconsistent with your schedule, just say so. This is the very last time I would be bringing the children back to you at any address other than your home (or the day-care in exceptional cases).

I need not emphasize on the fact that the children were in the same attire they were in on Friday at the day-care. You must be wondering, like me, why Flavie found being in her church with these children on Saturday evening (and perhaps Sunday too – the "somewhere" they had been invited to) more important to these children than spending a night with their father at whose place they last spent a night only in February 2015? I was enormously puzzling over this question (that evokes the same scenario like Scholastica's attitude while the London children were here in Montreal in March 2012[5]) and

---

5 See Fossungu, 2014: 124-25. During the February 2015 weekend they were with me, I ended up taking the Montreal children straight to the day-care on Monday morning. A little moment before the arranged time of my dropping them off at home, I called and Flavie said she wasn't yet at home but very close to it, promising to call me as soon as she gets home for me to bring them. Her close-to-home call came after 10.00 PM when I had already put the children to bed at about 8.45 PM. I told Flavie that I was not going

many more as the children took their long three-hour plus nap on that same Saturday. You may also be wondering about the long nap until you realize that I was quite aware that they might not even have a good sleep that particular night. For, when exactly were they to get home that night from the church? And also from the "somewhere" to which they were invited the next day? In short, even the day-care provider has never stopped complaining to me (both in person and on the phone) about their always being tired especially on the first few days following the weekend, due, certainly, to lack of enough sleep and rest. There are lots of other irregularities the day-care provider alleges, of course; and how it is very difficult dealing with their very disrespectful mother who does not stick to her words, how she (day-care provider) is only still having the children there just because of me, etc.

But isn't it justly amazing that the owner of an establishment like this that is well placed to acquaint the courts with all those testimonies would not be keen on going to court to testify? Wouldn't that alone have reduced all her complaints to me to mere *kongosa*? Having lived (and still living) all what the day-care provider complains about live, I personally know it is not just gossip, which leads me to the observation: Canadian institutions and children's best interests indeed! As I was reflecting while the children were napping, the idea of writing this book occurred to me because a very loud, clear and persistent voice inside my clock-ticking head just kept incessantly saying: "Don't relent in very piercingly speaking out for the children. You seem to be the only voice they now have." As you can visualize, that familiar inside-head voice was truly harping on the need for me to further speak out for the millions of children who are improperly suffering solely because of the scheming of their so-called parents, fortified by

---

to get them up then, indicating that she would only pick them from the day-care to where I would be taking them directly the next morning.

the complicity of Canadian institutions; establishments that are supposedly there to protect these same children. What a mess!

Here is how the rubbish is tackled in this book. Chapter 1 defines concepts and acquaints you with the facts of *Henriflavipeterism*, critically studying the Number One Lesson in the Child-Support Business School: always trying to discover if children, to the students and graduates of this School, are brought into the world for the sake of really having children or merely as money-getting tools. The second chapter discusses the various stages the case has (since the initial agreement) gone through until the March 2015 decision. It investigates into whether and how the gold-digging enterprise has successfully reversed gear to take Momany from the University of Windsor back to the forest, where the gold-diggers seem to think he properly belongs. Chapter 3 analyses the sole custody verdict in the context of children's best interest vis-à-vis Canadian institutions; this time square-pecking Citizenship and Immigration Canada (CIC) and its heartless officers who bluntly believe that children must go on forever carrying the cross for their parents' and the institutions' faulty reasoning.

Abbreviations

CCAS: Cameroon College of Arts and Sciences
CCTB: Canada Child Tax Benefits
CDN: Cote-Des-Neiges
CIBC: Canadian Imperial Bank of Commerce
CIC: Citizenship and Immigration Canada
CPC-M or CPCM: Case Processing Centre Mississauga
CSQ: *Certificat de Sélection du Québec*
CTV: Canadian Television
EI: Employment Insurance
FIO: Family Irresponsibility Office
FRO: Family Responsibility Office
GST/HST: Goods and Services Tax/Harmonized Sales Tax –
(TPS/TVH in French)
JCA: Joint Custody Agreement
IRB: Immigration and Refugee Bard
MLT: My Loose Translation
MYR: Aménagement MYR Inc.
ON: Ontario
PAF: Peter Ateh-Afac Fossungu
QC: Quebec
RFL: Report of Family Law
SCPCS: Shared Custody Plus Child(ren) Support
(decision)
SIN: Social Insurance Number
TPS/TVH: *Taxe sur les produits et services et taxe de vente harmonisée* – (GST/HST in English)

Chapter 1

Henriflavipeterism And The Number One Lesson In The Child-Support Business School: Children For Children Or Children For Money-Making Tools?

A Canadian of Cameroonian origin, I am personally incapable of hurting anyone. But my bitter truth does that 'hurting' all the time. I am known for embracing the bitter truth that many people can't just handle. That is even the main reason why I am still in Canada where I am hardly fitting in, and not in Cameroon where I *normally* would be, correctly educating the younger generation. I hardly fit in Canada not because I cannot fit into this great country. It is principally because Canada is yet to learn from the intriguing experiences and inter-cultural knowledge of some of its new citizens who, supposedly, do not have "Canadian Experience" (Fossungu, 2015a: x).

This chapter has two parts. This first part defines concepts and acquaints you with the facts of the case, including the movement from abduction to whitewashing illegality through *drunkabusivism*; while the second discusses the Joint Custody Agreement of January 30, 2013 – smoothly taking us into the next chapter which studies the various stages *Henriflavipeterism* has since gone through until the infamous March 2015 decision that chapter 3 then deciphers.

Suitactualization And Definitions: *Drunkabusivism* And *Sociowelfarism*

I have already told you in *Africans and Negative Competition in Canadian Factories* that I was in court in May 2014 not to argue with the law but solely to assist the court to reach a just

1

decision. I was there (as here) referring to a verdict that places the paramount interests of the children above all machinations from whatever source. Reference to children here does not mean just the two kids named in the *henriflavipeterist* utterly pointless suit. For those children's interests to be appropriately guaranteed, therefore, I was of the view that the Court was entitled to (and had to be given) all the essential facts, not the appearances. Against that background, I was therefore mostly spending time in that other book acquainting you with how and why the parties got to being in court (see generally Fossungu, 2015a: chapter 2). In that book I was giving you the facts of the case in a general manner. The facts of a case never change (except for liars) and are still good here. But to aid your trouble-free comprehension of the children-best-interest arguments of this book which solely hinges on the court's unusual sole custody verdict, I will need to clearly and pin-pointedly use the Affidavits of the parties in this Quebec case as well as the Ontario one.[1] The discussion in this section will be in two segments of (1) *Peterization* and (2) From Abduction to *Drunkabusivism*.

Peterizing the Court with an *Affidavit Détaillé Amendé*

Peterization (hereinafter Peter's Facts) is dated January 29, 2013 and composed of 83 paragraphs, the numbering of which will be referred to throughout this book. Essentially, it is affirmed that Peter is a Canadian citizen residing at 325-7225 Rue de Nancy in Montreal, having lived common law with Henriette-Flavie Bayiha since 2009 and having the two named children with her.[2] It is important to understand what being in

---

[1] See *Scholastica Achankeng Asahchop v Peter Ateh-Afac Fossungu*, London Family High Court, File N° 1162-05 (hereinafter *Asahchop v. Fossungu*).

[2] Peter's Facts, paragraphs 1-3.

a common law relationship means. So, I turn to the specialists who tell us the meaning of *come-we-stay* in these terms:

If you live or "cohabit" with someone without being married, people often say you are in a common law relationship or you are cohabiting. There is no single definition of what constitutes a common law spouse. For many Ontario laws you need to live together for three years or together be the parents of a child. For most federal laws, you are considered a common law couple if you live together for one year.

An important distinction between married and common law spouses is the right to property when the relationship breaks down. Couples who live together do not have the same rights as married couples to a share in the value of property, including the home they live in, unless the property is in both of their names.[3]

For some two or three months back Flavie had not been bothering whether or not the children ate, etc.; leaving the house in the morning (without telling anyone to where) and coming back late in the night. On arriving, she would disturb especially the sleeping children with her cell phone that rings twenty-four hours of the day. If Peter asked her to think of the children and inform those always calling her to choose appropriate times to do so, Peter was called a 'dictator' over and over. That it just got to a point that Peter had to tell Flavie that it was better for her to look for a different place to live in; one where she would assume no responsibility whatsoever, and where no one would ask her to respect simple rules. She asked for time to look for her apartment and the man gave her a month. But that period came and went, with Flavie behaving as if nothing mattered, and with the situation worsening by the day. Peter had to eventually go to the Regie de Logement and initiate the process for having Flavie leave the apartment

---

3   http://www.attorneygeneral.jus.gov.on.ca/english/justice-ont/family_law.asp

because the kids were hardly sleeping. On January 8, 2013 the eviction case was heard;[4] with the decision ejecting her from the apartment being rendered on January 29, 2013 (Fossungu, 2015a: 68). As part of the Regie expulsion process, we can see that on November 20, 2012 I had sent the following "NOTICE TO VACATE MY APARTMENT" by registered mail to Ms Bayiha:

> I had told you in a gentlemanly way that you leave my dwelling since you do not want to stay here on the terms on which you moved in; but you have been behaving as if I am such a foolish person. Take notice that you now have ten (10) days under article 1940 of the Quebec Civil Code to vacate my apartment. Do treat this matter with the urgency and importance that it merits.
> Thank you.
> Sincerely, Peter A. Fossungu, Dr.

In addition to the above facts, Peter claimed that he was better placed to carter for and assumed sole custody of the children because he works (although at that time he was on employment insurance due to the seasonal nature of his work) and have been the sole provider for the family.[5] Their mother, on the other hand, he asserted, does not work and earns no revenue, having herself recognized that she is incapable of taking care of the children and consenting that Peter be considered as the one having custody of them,[6] the more so as Flavie is not a landed immigrant and her status in Canada is precarious.[7] Moreover, in addition to asserting that she would happily sign the Consensual Agreement *"si ça va permettre à ces*

---

[4] Peter's Facts, paragraphs 4-9, 11 & 21-24.

[5] *Id.* paragraphs 25-28 & 14-15.

[6] *Id.* paragraph 13, & 16-17.

[7] *Id.*, paragraphs 76-77.

4

enfants de continuer à recevoir leur argent" (Fossungu, 2015a: 69), on November 29, 2012 Flavie also wrote the following note in French, addressed to Revenue Canada, that is found in the court suit as evidence: "Monsieur, Madame: Je tiens à vous informer pour le changement de l'état civil, actuel, concernant les prestations fiscales pour enfants. J'aimerai que cet argent soit versé à mon conjoint Mr PETER FOSSUNGU ATEH-AFAC, car il est entièrement responsable de la famille. Veuillez agréer, Monsieur, Madame nos salutations les plus meilleures. Signed. HENRIETTE FLAVI BAYIHA" Yet, at the last minute she refused signing the Consensual Agreement to that effect after ten days of consulting her social worker and lawyer.[8]

You can also get all this matter clearly from a letter I sent to Me. Jean-Marc Grenier on Sunday, December 30, 2012, in response to his request for information in connection with the signature status of the Agreement.

> Hi Me. Grenier:
> I got the package the next day, thanks.
> I handed the copies to Flavie the same day and she said she was going to sign after consulting with her social worker and lawyer. But until now (ten days later) she is saying nothing about it, despite the fact that she had agreed to have a consensual agreement on this matter. And, that is not all. She leaves the house in the morning and comes back close to midnight; and keeps disturbing the children (to leave myself out) from sleeping with her cell phone that just does not stop ringing and her phone conversations. Frankly, I am just so sick and tired of her comportment and want to get her out of my apartment as fast as possible; especially for the interest of the children.

---

[8] *Id.*, paragraphs 17-20.

I am assuming that she does not want things done consensually and we have therefore to proceed in the matter as such. I need an appointment with you as soon as possible after 1 January 2013.

The information requested is as follows:

My mother's name: FONGE, Regina Akiefac

My DOB: ... [omitted]

Flavie's mother's name: NGO BAYIHA, Rachel

Her DOB: ...... [omitted]

Her SIN: ..... [omitted]

Her cell phone: ... [omitted]

Thanks and seasons wishes to you.

Peter A. Fossungu

In view of all this, one cannot but be pushed to conclude that Flavie is not after what is best for the children. Much debate about child custody has focused upon criteria that courts use in awarding permanent physical custody in cases where two biological parents disagree. Noncustodial parents of both genders have long charged that judges' decision making is arbitrary and that it does not focus on the child. In response to this criticism, many American states have adopted a standard that places primary emphasis on the best interests of the child. The challenge for courts since the 1990s has been to interpret the standard objectively in the absence of meaningful guidelines.[9] It is true that the non-custodial parent in *Henriflavipeterism* claims that Flavie is just after the money and not the best interests of the children since (1) her work permit had expired in 2010 and it was not certain that she had then renewed it, (2) she has two other children in Cameroon and sends all the money that she receives here in Canada for our two children to Cameroon, (3) by regulation, she is not allowed

---

[9] http://legal-dictionary.thefreedictionary.com/Child+Custody.

to register the children in day-care.[10] Quite apart from my detailed analysis elsewhere (see Fossungu, 2015a: chapter 2), you can also see that money and free-riding are all what Flavie is about, and not the children's best interest, from the following events that abruptly transformed a consensual agreement to this infamous court case.

Sustaining the Free-Riding Enterprise: From Children Abduction to *Drunkabusivism* and *Sociowelfarism*

On Saturday, 19 January 2013 at about 9: 10 AM Flavie was served with documents for court hearing scheduled for January 30, 2013 and she threatened Peter (in French) with "You will see when I begin my own action."[11] On Tuesday, 22 January 2013 Peter picked up the children at day-care and by the time he returned Flavie was at home. This was about 5.45 PM and was very unusual because she was normally never back before 9.00 PM. She did not care to feed or bathe and change the children, but was busy with taking things in plastic bags out of the apartment, pretending all the time to be doing laundry with the elder child: all the while on her cellular phone with someone. Peter was still struggling to prepare the children for bed by feeding, changing them, etc. Remember that Flavie had all through her 'laundry show' been on the phone with someone who was to pick up "something" at her address. At about 7.00 PM Flavie put on the children's winter coats, saying they were going "somewhere". When Peter told her that she should be prepared to stay home when the children fall sick because of the cold weather she was taking them into, she said "someone" was picking them up, and then the doorbell rang. Peter objected to the children going anywhere that evening and undressed them of the coats and boots, asking Flavie to go to

---

10 Peter's Facts, paragraphs 78-81. See also Fossungu, 2015a: 30.

11 Peter's Facts, paragraphs 30-31.

her "somewhere" alone. Flavie never left the house to anywhere that night and the supposed laundry stuff never came back up to the apartment. She made sporadic movements in and out of the apartment; always on the phone with her "someone".[12]

Wednesday, 23 January 2013, was too cold and Peter called the day-care to let them know the children were staying home. Flavie never left the house that day as she did every day until then. All day she kept telling the children that she was going to Maxi to get this and that. She went out for a while and came back, complaining that she had forgotten the money, and keeping the Maxi-going tale alive. At about 6.00 PM she stepped out and came back with just a litre of milk and some meat and prepared some rice. This was very unusual for someone who, for the past four or so months, did not care about whether or not the children ate.[13] Just consider that evening's meal as the Last Supper and Judas' goodbye kiss, if you will.

Contextualizing the Police False and the Family Irresponsibility Office while *Drunkabusivistically* and Your-Honourably Whitewashing Illegality

On Thursday, 24 January 2013, it was still cold and Peter had no intention of taking the children to day-care. They were up and asking for banana, milk, cereal, etc. But there was none. Peter went out to see if the car would start and when it started he went back to the apartment to make sure there was enough time for him to run to Maxi and be back before 9.00 AM – the usual time Flavie often left the house. It was about 8.30 AM and Peter rushed to Maxi to grab a few items for the children, since he did not want to drag them into the cold after Flavie

---

[12] *Id.*, paragraphs 32-45.

[13] *Id.*, paragraphs 51-52.

must have gone. Peter was back from Maxi at about 8.55 AM and Flavie and the children were gone! He called the day-care and they were not there, with the day-care provider promising to call back as soon as they would arrive there. That call never came because they were never there that day (and until after the case in court, leading to shared custody). Peter then called Flavie's cellular phone which rang but she never answered. Since he waited in vain for her communication, Peter called the police between 11.00 AM and noon that day. The police came to the apartment and he gave them Flavie's cell phone number. One of the police officers (they were three, including a lady) got out of the apartment and called her while the other two remained in the apartment, sort of suspecting Peter for some foul play. Oh, the Police False and Blacks! You think it is only in the USA? The officer outside finally came back in and told Peter that the children and Flavie were in security (from what?) but that Peter could not be told where they were; and that Flavie would call him (Peter) later on. The police then left but Flavie never called Peter.[14]

The police agents were even very angry that I had wasted their time calling them there when the children were taken along by their mother who has all the right to be with them! There was just nothing wrong meriting my calling of 911, they reprimanded me. I nevertheless thanked them for coming because, with their intervention, I was then aware of the fact that my abducted children were alright. I then asked them if they would have believed me saying that I was not aware of the children's whereabouts if, say, that same evening it was discovered that something terrible had happened to them? All I got in response was "We are just doing our job." Doing their job indeed! What actually is their job?

It was the same reaction when I also had these uniform guys into my apartment in LaSalle sometime in 2001 when,

---

[14] *Id.*, paragraphs 53-71.

because I could see traces of blood here and there (like someone was menstruating) and my pregnant wife kept insisting that everything was okay. Led by Sergent-détective Bruce Houghton of Centre opérationnel Ouest and Constable P. Bigras, these guys immediately drove me out of the apartment before "having their talk" with Scholastica. I was then brought in and questioned why I called them there whereas Scholastica did not carry out an illegal (but lawful) abortion. After also thanking them for making me know about the abortion (whatever classification attached), I asked them as well if they would have believed me testifying that I had absolutely nothing at all to do with it if something went wrong during the said "lawful abortion"? Just doing our job, of course, is the sing-song for the hard *fossungupalogistic* quiz. And to the issue of a legally married woman single-handedly terminating a pregnancy at her own pleasure, the *police false* agents made this clear to me: "It is her body and she alone decides whether or not to have a pregnancy terminated." Children's best interest indeed! Yes Mr. Police False! That is certainly why these women know they can also do whatever they feel like doing with the un-terminated pregnancy (the excreted child), I guess? Would the Police False have reacted the same way if it was Flavie, for instance, who called them because I had done what she did? I need not say it; but you know as well as I do that I would have been in Prison Custody and also on CTV and all the other *dollarocratic* news media over and over and over as "The Father Who Abducted His Two Sons To Prevent Custody Being Granted To Their Mother". That is the Canadian Justice System indeed! A system that protects children a lot (only against their loving daddies, I guess)?

Having abducted the children as just outlined above in order to free-ride, there was then also the need to fabricate facts (nicely described as *affidavit circonstancié*[15]) so as to whitewash the illegality by painting the only capable parent as unfit and more. Flavie would thus affirm in her affidavit that she is the defendant; that she and Peter Ateh-Afac Fossungu have been living separated since 24 January 2013; that Peter had, since 31 December 2012, changed the locks of the apartment without giving her copies of the keys; and that life had become so intolerable with Peter that she had no choice but to take necessary action to make sure the children had *un endroit sûr*.[16] Yes, you can see her objective in now defining a shelter as being *un endroit sûr* than the 'uncertainty of a' home she and the children had been living in since 2009: simply because Peter has said 'No More' to her free-riding and unbecoming comportment. Thus, according to Flavie, Peter had tried to expel her from the apartment and she took refuge in a shelter (*un centre pour femmes en difficulté*) on 24 January 2013 where she could live for three months, being enough time for her to be able to find an apartment for herself; having already applied for social welfare.[17] Stating that the children were then not part of any court decision or an agreement with *un directeur de la protection de la jeunesse*, she claimed that she has always taken good care of the children since their birth, whereas Peter has always been absent for long periods since he works with Aménagement MYR in Dolbeau-Mistassini from May to October each year; concluding that the children were used to being with their mother and were then only 3 years and 16 months, respectively.[18]

Flavie considered Peter to be unfit to take care of the young children, with her being the best thing for them because

---

15 See Flavie's 26-paragraph *Affidavit Circonstancié* dated 30 January 2013.

16 *Id.*, paragraphs 1-2, 4 & 7.

17 *Id,* paragraphs 5-6 & 8.

18 *Id.*, paragraphs 3 & 9-10.

it is she who had been doing *everything* for them, including paying for day-care; and that she was soon to receive her renewed work permit and would work since she has already trained as a nurse-aid.[19] That was January 2013 she was making all this stuff about working soon. In March 2015 she is still to start working and yet gets full custody of the children like ABC, with the court's full knowledge that she is now on social welfare. And all that notwithstanding Peter's highlighted willingness and readiness to give up his more lucrative out-of-town job for any less-paying one in town in order to take proper care of the children on his proper earnings and efforts: in the event that he is accorded the sole custody he was also asking for. The March 6 (2015) court just did not listen to reason, for further reasons you will be immersed in as you read on into the hide and seek divorce/separation games.

The Quebec-Ontario Divorce Hide-and-Seek: Revenue Canada Does It Before the Courts?

Flavie has been out to copycat Scholalastica who seems to have been using the marriage like Collins' wife (see Fossungu, 2015a: 23-26 & 43-46). You could see this too in her never using the Fossungu surname; making it not surprising that the case is *Asahchop v. Fossungu* and not *Fossungu v. Fossungu* as most family cases appear.[20] You also realize that in her behaving all through as though we were already divorced (especially when I decided not to continue being around and taking 'all her shit'

---

[19] *Id.*, paragraphs 11-16.

[20] See, e.g., *Corbett v Corbett* (1970) 1 AER 943; *Dredge v. Dredge* (1947) 1 AER 29; *Bassett v. Bassett* (1975) 1 AER; and Ephraim N. Ngwafor, *Ngwafor's Law Students Examination Guide: Family Law* (Limbe: Jotan Printers, no year). For some Canadian examples, see *Philips v. Philips* 14 RFL (1995) 113 (Alberta Court of Appeal); *Harvey v. Harvey* 14 RFL (1995) 128 (British Columbia Court of Appeal); *MacNeil v. MacNeil* 14 RFL (1995) 24 (British Columbia Supreme Court); and *Couvillon v. Couvillon* 14 (1995) 316 (Ontario Family Court).

like Zimbabwe's Collins in in *Collinsianism*). Thus, I would get Revenue Canada telling me in a letter of October 3, 2003 that my marital status is 'Divorced'. My response to this craze was on October 13, 2003:

Dear Sir/Madam: I refer to your letter dated October 3, 2003. You state that my marital status is DIVORCED. That is not correct. I merely informed you of my change of address, indicating that I was not living at the current address [210-7110 CDN] with my wife and two children who are still at the old address. That is totally a different thing from saying that I was already divorced, or that I am no longer taking care of the two children. Do therefore base your review of my entitlement to the GST/HST credit on anything else but not on my being divorced. I am not and do not know when I ever told you I was divorced. Sincerely, signed. [Paragraphing altered]

The question any right-thinking person must be asking concerns why Revenue Canada could have changed my marital status without requiring the court decree of same? Could they just have taken the woman's word on the matter, as usual? It even gets more puzzling when, after all the talking above, on December 10, 2003 the Revenue Department wrote that:

This is in response to your letter dated October 13, 2003, regarding your marital status.

We are unable to fully process your request to change your marital status because it was incomplete.

Our records indicate that your marital status was 'divorced' on August 01, 2003.

Please provide the following information and return this letter to the address listed on the bottom of this page:

Your   current   marital   status:

_____

The   exact   date   your   marital   status   began:

_____

Your   ex-spouse/common-law   partner's   signature:

_____

Your   signature:

_____

If you have any further questions, please call 1-800-959-1953. Our website address is www.ccra.gc.ca should you require any additional information.

Yours sincerely,

(Signed)

Yvon Guerard

Benefit Program

When would wonders ever end in the Canadian bureaucracy? The same Revenue Canada would be inviting me over and over *sans cesser* to prove to them that I and Flavie are no longer living at the same address; and requiring the signatures of a whole list of persons (professionals) that must be in testimony of same: notwithstanding that I have all the court documentation sent to them showing that I am paying child support to her. The pestering just got to a point that I simply *lapidationistically* told them in a March 2015 letter to go to any comfortable hell they can find if they think that I am lying that I am no longer living with a woman to whom the courts are so silly to be requiring my making children support payments. Do these guys really comprehend what documents from other governmental departments mean? I guess they are just so bent on the *money* too that they think about nothing else. I guess my marital status and my language preference were switched at the same time; leading me to want to believe that (like Scholastica's case of divorce) monolingual Flavie is also behind the separation switching here.[21] Why? Because, since I

---

[21] The money for children from this Agency is such an enticing 'unearned' windfall to Flavie that she would do just about anything to lay her hands on it to send to Cameroon, of course. For instance, for just one child (Peter, Jr.) in the period of July 2009 to June 2010, she had paid to her

began getting the pestering from Revenue Canada, all communication has been in French, and I do not remember having ever changed my language of communication preference with this Agency.

Anyway, after my 'I-Don't-Care' *lapidationizing* note, on April 15, 2015 I received their letter of April 10, 2015 titled "Objet: crédit pour la taxe sur les produits et service et taxe de vente harmonisée (TPS/TVH)" which explained:

En nous fondant sur les résultats d'un récent examen, nous avons redressé votre état civil pour indiquer conjoint de fait pour l'année 2012 et séparé depuis janvier 2013.

Nous avons pris cette décision en nous fondant sur les éléments suivants :

Vous avez indiqué que vous et votre époux (se) ou conjoint(e) de fait avez continué ou recommencé à vivre ensemble dans le même logement. Lorsqu'un couple continue ou recommence à vivre ensemble dans le même logement et continue de partager les responsabilités parentales et/ou financières, nous ne considérons pas la séparation comme ayant eu lieu aux fins de l'administration de la prestation fiscale canadienne pour enfants et du crédit pour la taxe sur les produits et service/taxe de vente harmonisée (TPS/TVH), même si vous vous considériez comme colocataires.

Nous vous enverrons, au besoin, des avis officiels expliquant les rajustements apportés à vos prestations et à vos crédits pour enfants et familles ainsi qu'à vos cotisations d'impôt.

Si vous nous envoyez des renseignements supplémentaires, nous examinerons votre compte....

M. Charland

---

the sum of $1423.30. See Revenue Canada letter to her dated 20 avril 2010. Imagine then what the amount would be since the arrival of Peteraf in 2011 and you have got the perfect money-equation behind *Henriflavipeterism*; as well as the CCTB note that was written by her but never sent to Revenue Canada.

Did they really need my angry and *lapidationistic* letter in order to offer the above explication? Here they have court papers and others indicating my separation from a woman and would still be demanding proof of my separation. But they changed my status from 'married' to 'divorced' without my request, nor requiring the divorce decree, nor even the signatures that they now must need to be able to complete the process of reverting it from *divorced* to *married*? Should I not take it that Scholastica had already secretly divorced me without my knowledge in Centre fiscal Shawingan-Sud (Québec) before the charade in London, Ontario? Divorced twice by the same wife! I must surely enter the Book of World Records as well as the Marriage Failures Hall of Fame at the same time as the Family Courts of this country are finding their merited place in the Hall of Shame. True, because the London Court was just wasting time and tax-payers' money doing what it did: the more so as the above letter from Revenue Canada was tendered in the court file in question. Do these courts too ever read all the stuff the parties put forward as evidence? I don't think so. And the following is why, in addition.

In the *Asahchop v. Fossungu* case in my **Form 13 – Financial Statement** (Support Claims) (page 6) I clearly ticked the box that says 'I do expect changes in my financial situation as follows': My reasons were two, namely, "(1) For health and other medical considerations, I do not expect to continue doing two jobs till the end of 2006. (2) I expect to eventually

---

[22]MLT: It is basically saying that when they decide who is separated or married, for purposes of determining one's entitlements to child tax benefits, goods and services tax returns, etc., the Revenue Department does not consider couples that begin living together again as having been separated – even if they have resumed living together as co-tenants. In this case their previous separation is never considered as affecting their status.

get a professional job in my field of study." That Form was sworn before a Commissioner for taking affidavits in London, Ontario on August 28, 2006. I wonder if the London judges ever paid any attention to this information when they were making their decisions on the amount of child support I was to be paying to Scholastica. The more especially so as my letter of March 17, 2007 (faxed to the Court before Judge Vogelsang's Endorsement of March 20, 2007) made it clear that my total employment income for 2006 was **$38,418.47.**

The amount of $38,418.47 is clearly below the $41,473 that the judge would discretionarily impute as my 2006 income (see chapter 3 for more). But let's not concentrate on the child support itself here and rather do focus on the criminal means employed to get it, with the complicity of the courts that are so trigger-happy to nail the payer that the family irresponsibility office immediately also brands as the *debtor*. When Scholastica left Montréal for London in September 2004 to start working professionally as a social worker, I had to embark on working nights and days (two jobs) in order to pay back some of the astronomical debts I had contracted in order to educate and bring her to Canada, as well as eliminate outstanding bills. But the next thing I knew was that she had taken me to court in London (Ontario) in 2005, lying and asking for child support, child custody (and divorce). I put divorce in brackets because it was only in the London court house that I realized divorce was part of the package. But let us first get what happened before I ever got to the court myself, to understand how these women always try to trick both the Canadian institutions they are using and the person they are sucking the money out of.

When I got the "Form 39: Notice of Approaching Dismissal" signed on March 10, 2006 by L. McClintock (clerk of the court), I sent the following letter of March 16, 2006 titled "Re: Court File Number FC-05-001162-00" and got no response:

17

Dear Clerk of the Court, Yesterday evening (16 March 2006) I received *Form 39: Notice of Approaching Dismissal* that you signed on 10 March 2006 and in which I am named as Respondent, with Scholastica Achankeng Asahchop of 253 Blackacres Blvd, London, Ontario, as the Applicant. A lot of things are not clear to me respecting the above Court File.

The first issue concerns the address of the Applicant. On the date of signing *Form 39*, the Applicant's address that I have on file for mailing monthly cheques and other papers is: 1765 Attawangaron Rd, London, ON CA N6G 3M9 Tel.: (519) XXX-XXXX (omitted).

Second, my name and address are wrong in *Form 39*. These are items that are always duly indicated in areas of "Return Address" in all my mails to the Applicant and should be corrected as shown above.

Third, I have never been served with the Applicant's document of claim in **Court File Number FC-05-001162-00** in any of the ways in sub-rule 6(19) (a)-(d) of the *Family Law Rules*. If there has been a returned postcard as per sub-rule 6(19) (c), I do not know. I am therefore not aware "of all the issues in this case" and, consequently, not able to avoid dismissal of the case by taking any of the three actions mentioned in sub-rule 39(11) of the *Family Law Rules* that is duly cited in the *Form 39* in my possession. I would very much appreciate being duly acquainted with "all the issues in this case" so that I can clearly know what is going on and also be able to do what I can to avoid "a final order disposing of all the issues in this case".

Sincerely,

Peter Ateh-Afac Fossungu, LL.D.

The whole idea of the Applicant was to have her desires quickly granted without me being able to be present to present contrary facts. You see this also in the 'doctored' documents I was eventually served with that did not include divorce (Of course, she was surely not about to divorce me for the second time, I should assume?). I made the point to the court but it coolly ignored it since the original documents in the file were clear on, and included, the divorce point. The fact that the original document included the issue was no reason at all for the London Court to have overlooked the serious issues I raised in my expression of concerns which I also find necessary to lay here in its entirety, for a better understanding of both the divorce palaver and the mockery of the Canadian family court system. On this and other matters, I stated to the Court as follows.

In *Asahchop v. Fossungu*, on page 2 of my **Form 10 – Answer,** I ticked box 4, meaning "I am making a claim of my own" and box 5, indicating that "The FAMILY HISTORY, as set in the application is not correct." For the attachment required by box 4, I attached my claim titled "WHEN WAS THE RESPONDENT ACTUALLY SERVED BY THE APPLICANT? EXPLAINING THE APPARENT LATENESS IN MY ANSWER" which read:

It is now clear that the Applicant started a Divorce/Child Support/Custody of Child(ren) Case against me – the Respondent – on 15 July 2005. But it is not pellucid, first, **why** I was not served in time despite the fact that the Applicant had ample opportunities to do so even in person; and, second, **when I was served** – if at all – by the Applicant and **with what**.

On 16 March 2006, I received, in the mail, *Form 39: Notice of Approaching Dismissal*, signed on 10 March 2006 by L. McClintock (Clerk of the Court). I was in the dark and consequently wrote back to the Court (duly copying the Applicant by mail) requesting clarification to no avail.

On the weekend of 1 April 2006, I was with the Applicant in London, Ontario – attending our son's third birthday – and nothing about the case was mentioned to me.

On the long weekend of 8 April 2006, I was again in London, Ontario, spending the entire long weekend with our two children while the Applicant spent some time away from home. Again, nothing regarding the case or even my letter to the Court (a copy of which was sent to her) was talked of.

On 7 July 2006, (as per plan) the Applicant drove with our two children to Montreal where these children were to spend two weeks of their holiday with me. The following day (8 July 2006) we were all at Gatineau – Applicant, Respondent and two children – for a community event. Nothing on the subject of the case brought against me was mentioned.

On 21 July 2006, I took over the two children back to London, Ontario, as per plan. We arrived at about 10.20 p.m. While at her residence that evening (about 11 p.m.), the Applicant made me sign a consent portion of Change of Child(ren)'s Name Forms in which she had clearly answered "No" to a question seeking to know if the child(ren) is/were the subject of any legal proceedings. Having gone through the filled out forms and signed the portion reserved for me, she collected and stored them. Then, surprisingly to me, and with a kind of victorious smile on her face, the Applicant handed a bunch of papers to me, stating that these were court documents. I told her that whatever they were I was only going to look at them when I reach Montreal and then said goodbye to all three of them and headed for Montreal, Quebec.

Reaching home the next day, I discovered the documents the Applicant had handed to me to be:

i)   *Form 8: Application (General)*, dated 15 July 2005; and

ii) *Form 13: Financial Statement (Support Claims) Sworn/Affirmed*, dated 20 July 2006.

On page 4 of the copy of the Applicant's *Form 8* that I was served with on 20 July 2006, **Claims under the Divorce Act** are left blank. The only claims she made in the document are under the **Family Law Act or Children's Law Reform Act**, namely (1) Support for Child(ren) – Other than Table Amount and (2) Custody of Child(ren). This document has been quite puzzling to me. Why just these two issues and not also the main issue of divorce from which these other two take their roots?

On Saturday 19 August 2006 I received (by registered mail) a copy of the Applicant's requested Case Conference billed for 20 September 2006 (which is signed and dated 27 July 2006) to deal with the following issues: "child Support, Custody of Children". No divorce is again mentioned. Having made several failed attempts to get to the bottom of the puzzle through a Montreal-based lawyer (I am sure his communications to this Court are on file), I decided that it was high time I put the neglected main issue of divorce also into the picture.

On 21 July 2006 (the supposed deadline for my Answer to be in) I was at the Court House on 80 Dundas Street, London, Ontario, to agree with the Applicant's claims while also making a claim of my own touching on divorce and access to child(ren). My Answer/Application was rejected because, as the Family Court official attending to me explained, I could not be filing for divorce as the Applicant had already done so on 15 July 2006. Stupefied, I tried explaining that there was an error, showing her the copy of the Applicant's claims that I had. The official, on her part, pulled out the original copy of *Form 8* from File Number F1162/05 and spread page 4 before me to read for myself. I asked if I could have a copy of the document and the lady gladly made one for me and even advised me to see a duty counsel.

In the authentic *Form 8* that I obtained at the Court House on 21 August 2006, the Applicant clearly claimed **under the Divorce Act** for (00) Divorce, (03) Support for Child(ren) – other than table amount, and (04) Custody of Child(ren); and **under the Family Law Act or Children's Law Reform Act** for (12) Support for Child(ren) – other than table amount, and (13) Custody of Child(ren). Now, some serious and important

21

questions do necessarily arise. For example, when was the Respondent actually served and with what? What is the Applicant trying to hide from the Court and/or the Respondent by serving the Respondent, first, very reluctantly and, second, with only a somewhat doctored copy of her claims? Is there any reason for the Respondent to hereafter trust other documents – official and unofficial – that come through or from the Applicant (such as her *Form 13* with me that has a lot of blank spaces)?

So, tell me, was Scholastica actually after divorcing me in London (for a second time) or just after something else (the money) when, the doctored documentation issue apart, her "eyes and ears" are always nosing around in my regard? And also when, for more than six years, the divorce decision seemed to have been a forgotten issue with only the child support *amount* always being revisited by her? For example, on 21 October 2008, I wrote to the court asking to know about "what has happened or is happening to the divorce issue." I have pleaded on several other occasions, including on 28 September 2011, which made it clear that

I am the Respondent in Court File N° FC-05-001162-00 and writing to find out what has become of the divorce issue that the Applicant (Scholastica Asahchop) demanded together with the child support and custody that she has, since 26 September 2006 (date of The Honourable Madam Justice Blishen's judgment), been enjoying.

On 20 March 2007 Justice Henry Vogelsang in his Endorsement stated, regarding the divorce issue, that "… A judgment dissolving the marriage will issue in the usual form." It has been four years (since that endorsement) and seven years (since the cessation of cohabitation) but I am still to have the judgement dissolving the marriage.

I have to move on with my life and, as you can see from the birth documents enclosed, I cannot legally marry the mother of Peter Ateh-Afac Fossungu, Jr. & Peteraf Karlemon

Fossungu or anyone else until my marriage to Scholastica Asahchop has been legally ended. Two years separation alone is cause for divorce; five years separation alone is cause for divorce; but above all else the Applicant demanded in 2005 that the marriage be dissolved and the Respondent did not oppose it. So what is keeping this Court until now from doing just that? Please, I really need to carry on with my life and am here earnestly requesting that the judgement dissolving the marriage be issued as quickly as possible.

Thank you for your comprehension
Sincerely yours,
Peter Ateh-Afac Fossungu

Every time I wrote I was always told to get a lawyer to represent me on the matter. What bullshit! I even tried using the services of UTKDS (Untietheknot.ca) in 2011-2012 to speed up the untying. But they eventually cancelled and returned my $242.95 money order and the entire application because my case was truly above their untying power: since, according to their explanation, I did not have an Ontario address like the Applicant! So why did that Ontario Court not also refuse hearing the case on that score? Truly frustrated as I was, on April 8, 2013, I again sent the court this letter (RE: COURT FILE N° FC-05-001162-00), reiterating that

I am the Respondent in the abovementioned case (*Scholastica Asahchop v. Peter Ateh-Afac Fossungu*). I am writing again to find out what has happened or is happening to the divorce issue. Justice Vogelsang's Endorsement dated March 20, 2007 noted in paragraph (1) that "This brief divorce trial featured little real contest." In paragraph (2) it stated that "A judgment dissolving the marriage will issue in the usual form." This is 8 April 2013 and I have not heard anything regarding this matter. Can I please know what is still holding back the legal and formal dissolution of the marriage? Or could the judgment dissolving the marriage have been sent to another address? I really need to move on with my life. Thank you for a prompt response. Sincerely, Peter Ateh-Afac Fossungu." (Paragraphing altered)

Sometime afterwards I received a copy of the final judgement dated in October 2012 that was still bearing my Rue Sax address despite that I have always updated the court with my change of address. What is it with these Canadian institutions and children's best interest? Does the interest of children mean anything to them really? Although my financial position was then so disturbing, I could still have conveniently stopped Scholastica from taking the children to London, if I did not have their interest and future at heart. There are many reasons but just a few would suffice here. First, apart from her bearing them for nine months in the womb, these children, until their departure for London, knew no other parent than me because only their mother's schooling and taking care of her brothers, sisters, and parents was the most precious thing to her. Second, I had been the only one taking care of the family of four till that moment. And, third, being Quebecers, it would have been extremely hard for Scholastica to justify taking them out of Québec in any Québec court when their father wanted to continue staying with them in the province. In addition, there was my financial situation that, without the prime interest of the children at heart, should have been a great motivation for me to fight to keep them and claim child support from professionally-working Scholastica, *à la manière de* Capa-Mali (see Fossungu, 2015a: 39-41).

I am very sure this exacting prospect crossed Scholastica's mind when she was incessantly making her gratuitous swearing to a lot of people. I well remember her numerous *2001-2002* phone conversations with several people, while I was sitting right there. She told them that she would do *everything* possible to make sure that if she should not be the one to have these children, she would ensure that I would not be the one to have

24

them. Why would she be saying this unless (she and) her parents had already planned the 2005 court battle before then? Does that not also ally the Revenue Canada divorce above? This swearing conversation became almost incessant. But I particularly noted it twice: one with her cousin (Quinta Asaah, now in Calgary but) at that time based in Montréal, Canada; and the other with her friend (Relindis Nkafu Amingwa) in Maryland, USA. These two instances are special because, not only could I actually identify the others on the other end but I also did mark down the period of the conversation (time, day, month, and year). Now, the important question to answer concerns the type of parent that really loves her/his children but would rather prefer that they grow up in a public institution or foster home than with the other parent. It is for the same reasons of being aware of what was up against the future of the children that I also did not contest her court claims for child support, custody, and divorce. Has her student called Flavie not also learnt to do a good job at the Child-Support Business School?

Just reading through Flavie's *affidavit circonstancié*, it is very evident that it was a last minute desperate attempt to twist the plain facts that were advanced by the other side. For instance, while demanding *que Monsieur me remette mes effets personnels ainsi que ceux des enfants*,[23] listen to her funny justification for her comportment that led Peter to ask her to leave the apartment: I came back one day after midnight and Monsieur refused opening the door and I had to spend the night in the stairs of the building. *"De plus, en réponse au paragraphe 3, il est vrai que je quitte le logement après le départ des enfants, depuis que Monsieur est sur l'assurance emploi, pour ne pas être toute la journée avec lui. Pendant la journée je visitais mes amies, dont une viens d'accoucher et j'allais à l'Église prier. Je revenais pour le coucher des enfants."*[24] Quite apart

---

[23] Flavie's Affidavit, paragraph 17.

[24] *Id.*, paragraphes 18-20 & 22.

from the *eglise*-bullshit, Flavie certainly prefers taking care of someone else's new-born to staying at home and cooking for her own two sons who would return every day from day-care with no mother there to welcome them. The fittest parent for sole custody indeed to the *gravelling* and *zigzagging* Quebecois family court!

You wouldn't believe Flavie's talk of being locked out and my attempts to expel her from my apartment: just knowing that this is even the same Flavie who had thrown me out of "her" apartment without any notice in April 2012 (see Fossungu, 2015a: 65-66). As part of her 'Heightened Provoking Comportment' (Fossungu, 2015a: 67-73), Flavie once grabbed me on the neck (in the manner Cameroonians describe as *E don bottin me*), obviously expecting this foolish me to lay my hands on her and get quickly arrested. She never got that because she could simply not if the teacher, with more experience and tact, could not have. You get details of Scholastica's failure in the turn-him-into-a-prisoner tactics from my Letter of September 27, 2002 to her (titled 'Re: Support for Children'):

Scholastica, Enclosed you will find two cheques, each in the amount of a hundred and fifty dollars ($150), being support for Ngunyi and the unborn baby for the months of October and November 2002. Cheques for subsequent months will follow.

Well, I am really sorry that it has come to this but I guess that is what you have been looking for. I have been quietly taking all the "crab" you've been telling people on the phone, in my presence, about me. You have several times provoked me in such a way I should become violent toward you. I never was. Therefore you changed your strategy and became physically violent toward my person. Last Saturday, September 21, 2002, you attacked me on my neck while I was lying on the sofa. I struggled and got free of your assault. The next day, Sunday 22 September 2002, you were on the phone telling your

26

cousin, Quinta Asaah, that I kicked your stomach on Saturday. Incorrect. Assuming that I kicked you (not on the stomach), why didn't you also tell your cousin what happened to prompt the kick?

On Sunday 22 September 2002, you threatened me, prohibiting me from touching anything like food in the house because you were the one who bought it [for the very first time]. You went on the phone, as usual, to repeat and reiterate the threat and prohibition to your cousin, Quinta Asaah. You told her a lot of other things about me as I sat there. How would you feel living in a house where you cannot open the fridge and get anything out of it to eat? How would you feel feeding a child every evening with food that you yourself cannot taste?

All in all, I have realized that, by moving out, as I have done, I avoid being moved out into prison. I want to be part of our children's lives. I don't want to be locked up behind bars while they grow up. I could bear your insults quietly but I am not sure I can be physically attacked by you without reacting. And I know my self-defence will always be considered not as such in this society. That is why I think it is better, painful as it is to the children, to stay away from your assaults, though not completely away from the family. Sincerely, signed.

For the student's case, I later on called the police in to get Flavie out in order to prevent any further escalation of things. The police arrived and, after my narration, asked: "Was there violence?" and then made it clear to me that they cannot ask her to leave the apartment because she has the right to stay there even as the lease clearly shows only my name on it. So, you evidently are seeing that these uniformed gangsters are not there to prevent violence but to encourage, promote and *malo-racialize* it. You are still wondering what I mean and if that is even all of it? Then imagine where exactly I (a black man) would be today if it was Flavie who had called the *police false* after my violent reaction to her *bottining me*. If you are still not sure, then go back to her children abduction above; or you may instead cement it with this letter of August 19, 2008 titled "ACCESS TO CHILDREN DENIED" that I sent to Ontario's FIO (let them not continue fooling you that it is FRO), an integral part of the Ministry of Community and Social Services:

Dear Sir/Madam, I am writing to let your Office know that I am being denied access to my children. For the past two months or so I have not been able to talk to the children because their phone number had been changed without my knowledge of the new one. I have even tried several times communicating with their mother through email but have so far heard nothing from her. It is my belief that the Family Responsibility Office (FRO) is there to enforce the rights and obligations of all the parties, not just those of the Applicant alone.

Sincerely,

Peter A. Fossungu

I should not be the only one telling you here that the FIO (true to its name), like the Montreal Police False (don't be deceived here too that it is Force), didn't see that I and the children had any rights here. But just wait until you hear and see in the next chapter what their nationwide trigger-happy reaction is when the women (falsely or truthfully) would grumble about child support non-payments. You see this family gender-bias even in the court itself that tends to refuse to move past what the critics describe as the silly idea of always "award[ing] custody of young boys and of girls of all ages solely to mothers on the presumption that mothers are inherently better caretakers of young children."[25] I have nothing against the millions of exemplary mothers around the globe who truly

---

[25] http://legal-dictionary.thefreedictionary.com/Child+Custody

merit both the presumption and Prince Nico Mbarga' *Sweet Mother*. Remember that this *halfotwof* Cameroonian-Nigerian singing star also immortalized *Good Father* (even as not all of them are *good*).

Thus, realizing perhaps that all the hurriedly conjured up claims would not be enough to secure Flavie's welfare and other schemes, the father of the children just had to be damaged completely, to the extent that any right-thinking person must simply be doubting if it is the same person who fathers said children, and the same person who entered countless times between the woman's legs, evidence of which would be the children in question. Was the entry-permit only granted because the *mblacaus* (or penis) in there could not be avoided in the business of creating the money-making tools called children? Yeah! You got that right! Money-making from love-making! That appears to be the Number One Lesson in the Child-Support Business School. Otherwise, you could then easily sense that Flavie was just being couched by "someone" who, of course, would not have been given the true facts. Hence, the incoherence as we hear her stating that she refused to sign the Consensual Agreement prepared by Me. Jean-Marc Grenier because "I am not in agreement that Monsieur should have custody of the children."[26] How different, if at all, is this from Scholastica vowing to have the children in a public institution rather have them with me? I need not separately describe Flavie's surprise and wonder when she saw a copy of her own note addressed to Revenue Canada in the court file. Just put it alongside that of her teacher, Scholastica, when she too found out that I had become a permanent resident of Canada: despite all her road blocks (see Fossungu, 2014: 82).

So, how was Flavie to then explain her note of 28 November (that she herself had written voluntarily to Revenue Canada) in the context of her refusal to sign? She states:

---

[26] Flavie's Affidavit, paragraph 21.

"Quand [sic] à la lettre du 28 novembre pour les prestations fiscales c'était ce que le fonctionnaire du gouvernement fédéral m'avait demandé de faire pour qu'on puisse recevoir à nouveau les prestations."[27] (*As to the CCTB note, I wrote it because an agent of Revenue Canada had explained to me that it was what I needed to do so that the children's money could be reinstated.*) Meaning? This is the first interpretation. That she never actually sent the note to them because, otherwise, I would not have Revenue Canada pestering me until date with what my marital status is, as seen above. Canadian institutions always take the woman's word for the Gospel Truth, legal documentation furnished or not. Consequently, second, there should have been no need for the Consensual Agreement that her last-minute rejecting to sign dragged us to court. And, third, if she is not the one to receive the money and send to Cameroon as usual, no one else should: since "perpetual liars must obviously be thinking always that everyone else is lying to them" (Fossungu, 2015a: 70). Otherwise, the question remains: Does her explanation just make any sense? And was she not then seeking the court order for sole custody (that she obtained on March 6, 2015) just for the sole purpose of laying her hands on that money? Money-only sole custody, says even her *gravelling* lawyer! Scholastica too got me divorced before Revenue Canada for exactly the same reason, I should guess? But, wanting to sucker money also from me directly, the London Court had to be used for that purpose: even if it meant illegally divorcing me twice but still putting my life on hold for close to eight years.

Flavie too wanted the Revenue Canada money at all costs and any sort of lie that would get her there is in place, even if it also means committing perjury as she did in countless occasions: with the Quebec *zigzagging* court not also bothering about it. It is just as the *police false* did not see anything wrong with her children abduction because, as they proudly put it,

---

[27] *Id.* paragraph 24.

"she is the mother of the children" and that "it is her body" (for the abortionist). Sexist law and its father-killing/abusing application in Canada, isn't it? To reiterate, just imagine where I would be today if I was the one comporting myself in Flavie's shoes! And here comes what she and her *gravelling* counsellors must have devised as the last joker-card to the free-riding enterprise. I am talking about *drunkabusivism* that you get from her Affidavit's paragraph 23: *"Monsieur est venu à plusieurs réprises au petit matin en état d'ébriété avancé. Il a même une fois été malade de boisson dans sa voiture au mois de novembre 2012"*. I just don't need to refute this nonsense here again (see Fossungu, 2015a: 50-55), preferring to use precious space and time discussing the joint custody accord.

The Joint Custody Agreement of January 30, 2013: Reigning Unperturbed Until September 2013

Child custody is the care, control, and maintenance of a child, which a court may award to one of the parents following a divorce or separation proceeding. Under most circumstances, we are told, U.S. state laws provide that biological parents make all decisions that are involved in rearing their child: such as residence, education, health care, and religious upbringing. Parents are not required to secure the legal rights to make decisions if they are married and are listed in the child's birth certificate. However, if there is disagreement about which parent has the right to make these decisions, or if government officials believe that a parent is unfit to make the decisions well, then family courts or juvenile courts will determine custody. We cannot proceed here except by examining all the forms of custody: joint, shared, sole, and split. It is important to attempt a distinction of them first. As we are told,

31

- Joint custody means that both parents make major decisions about the children together.
- Sole custody means that one parent makes all major decisions about the children.
- Children's living arrangements can vary greatly. In some cases children maintain a primary residence with one parent and visit regularly with the other. In others the children divide their time equally or approximately equally between the parents' homes.
- Shared custody exists when children live with each parent at least 40 per cent of the time. In these circumstances, special provisions apply to the calculation of child support, depending on the amount of time children spend with each parent.[28]
- Split custody is an arrangement in which the parents divide custody of their children, with each parent being awarded physical custody of one or more children. In general, courts try not to separate siblings when awarding custody.[29]

I have two children with my ex-partner and, as you already know, we separated in late January 2013. On January 30, 2013 there was a Mutual Agreement made in court giving both of us shared custody, with each party paying day-care for a child.[30]. This JCA (Joint Custody Agreement) could be what has been referred to as joint or shared custody. It was arrived at in this case because of some interesting facts. I who was (and still am) obviously better suited to having sole custody of the children, worked out-of-town. Flavie was then having the children physically but had (and still has) a precarious situation in

---

28   http://www.attorneygeneral.jus.gov.on.ca/english/justice-ont/family_law.asp

29 http://legal-dictionary.thefreedictionary.com/Child+Custody

30 See Consentement Interimaire sur Requéte pour Garde d'Enfants, as endorsed by Procès-Verbal d'Ordonnance de Sauvegarde in the presence of Me. Daniele Besner (greffière spéciale) and Jessy Villalta (greffière) [hereinafter JCA].

Canada, not being a permanent resident or citizen. Therefore, the compromise reached by the parties through their lawyers was the mutually agreed upon JCA of January 30, 2013. By this JCA, Flavie has the children during the months (22 May-6 October) that I am away working and I take over when I am back in town (7 October-21 May). That was the rationale behind the 4/3-3/4 alternative weekly formula of joint custody – with each parent paying day-care for one child. There was no children support involved. But, although lie-telling Flavie will naturally dispute it, I still often sent her money while in Dolbeau-Mistassini: since I was quite aware of the fact that she never likes to fend for herself, consequently making uncertain the children's feeding, clothing, etc. If Flavie is truthful at all, she would easily recount and attest to the fact that I also always did shopping for them whenever I happened to come to Montreal, for any reason – short break, *arrêt-feu*, you name it.

All this happening largely because the only reason I wanted Flavie out of my residence and life was the best interest of the children (I mean all of her four children); and not that she should be completely out of the lives of the two here in Canada or be furnishing me with any child support money whatsoever. Child support was never (and still is not) an option when I initially asked for custody of the children, explaining why my REQUÉTE POUR GARDE ET ORDONNANCE DE SAUVEGARDE (ART. 600, 604 ET 605 C.C.Q ET 813.3 ET 813.9 C.P.C) of January 15, 2013 enumerated most of what you already know from *Peterization*, and concluded with:

PAR CES MOTIFS, PLAISE AU TRIBUNAL:

[1] ACCUEILLIR la présente requête; [2] ACCORDER la garde légale et physique des enfants mineurs parties…. au requérant; [3] ORDONNER à l'intimée de quitter le 7225, rue de Nancy #325, à MONTREAL, QUÉBEC, (H3R 2L8) dans les dix (10) jours du jugement à intervenir; [4]ACCORDER à l'intimée, lorsqu'elle aura un logement convenable, les droits de visites et de sorties selon l'entente, à défaut d'entente, l'intimée

aura les droits suivants: a) Une (1) fin de semaine sur deux (2), à compter du vendredi soir 18h00 au dimanche soir 18h00, incluant les jours de congé des enfants précédant ou suivant ses fins de semaines ; b) L'intimée aura les enfants pour une période de sept (7) jours consécutifs durant la période des vacances de Noël des enfants, incluant alternativement chaque année le jour de Noël ou le Jour de l'An à commencer par le jour de Noël 2012; c) Pendant la période estivale, l'intimée aura les enfants avec elle deux (2) semaines consécutives ou non, durant ses vacances estivales, l'intimée devant aviser le requérant un (1) mois à l'avance pour lui indiquer quelles seront ses deux (2) semaines; d) Lesdits droits d'accès seront effectués de façon à ce que le requérant ait les enfants la fin de semaine de la Fête des Pères et que l'intimée ait les enfants la fin de semaine de la Fête des Mères; [5] PRENDRE ACTE que l'intimée ne paiera pas au requérant une pension alimentaire pour les enfants car elle n'a, actuellement aucune revenu; [6] ORDONNER à l'intimée d'informer le requérant sans délai: a) lorsqu'elle aura trouvé un lieu pour vivre et de transmettre ses coordonnées; b) lorsqu'elle aura une source de revenu en indiquant qui est le payeur et ses coordonnées; c) lorsqu'elle aura trouvé un travail en lui indiquant le nom de son employeur, ses coordonnées ainsi que son salaire hebdomadaire brut et net; ORDONNANCE DE SAUVEGARDE DURANT L'INSTANCE, LE REQÉERANT DEMANDE: [7] ACCORDER la garde légale et physique des enfants mineurs parties.... au requérant; [8] ORDONNER à l'intimée de quitter le 7225, rue de Nancy #325, à MONTRÉAL, QUÉBEC, (H3R 2L8) dans les dix (10) jours du jugement à intervenir; [9]ACCORDER à l'intimée, lorsqu'elle aura un logement convenable, les droits de visites et de sorties selon l'entente, à défaut d'entente, l'intimée aura les droits suivants: a) Une (1) fin de semaine sur deux (2), à compter du vendredi soir 18h00 au dimanche soir 18h00, incluant les jours de congé des enfants précédant ou suivant ses fins de semaines ; b) L'intimée aura les enfants pour une période de sept (7) jours consécutifs durant la période des vacances de Noël des enfants, incluant alternativement chaque année le jour de Noël ou le Jour de l'An à commencer par le jour de Noël 2012; c) Pendant la période estivale, l'intimée aura les enfants avec elle deux (2) semaines consécutives ou non, durant ses vacances estivales, l'intimée devant aviser le requérant un (1) mois à l'avance pour lui indiquer quelles seront ses deux (2) semaines; d) Lesdits droits d'accès seront effectués de façon à ce que le requérant ait les enfants la fin de semaine de la Fête des Pères et que l'intimée ait les enfants la fin de semaine de la Fête des Mères; [10] PRENDRE ACTE que l'intimée ne paiera pas au requérant une pension alimentaire pour les enfants car elle n'a, actuellement aucune revenu; [11] ORDONNER à l'intimée d'informer le requérant sans délai: a) lorsqu'elle aura trouvé un lieu pour vivre et de transmettre ses coordonnées; b) lorsqu'elle aura une source de revenu en indiquant qui est le payeur et ses coordonnées; c) lorsqu'elle aura trouvé un travail en lui indiquant le nom de son employeur, ses coordonnées ainsi que son salaire hebdomadaire brut et net; [12] TOUT SANS FRAIS, sauf contestation.[31]

Paragraphing has obviously been altered and, as you can also see, paragraphs 7 to 11 are just repetitions, *à l'avocat*, of some previous paragraphs. It should be noted that paragraphs 11 and/or 6 are not intended to subvert paragraphs 5 and 10 later, but solely to make sure that Flavie actually *gets off her butt*

---

[31] MLT: Basically, it is saying that, while Peter requests to have sole custody of the children, he does not intend to keep their mother away from them because she would have all the access to them that she wants as soon as she has found a suitable accommodation for herself. It also demands that she communicates her contact information to Peter, that she gets a regular job for herself and let Peter also know the employer's contact information as well as Flavie's weekly remuneration. And, above all, it emphasizes that Peter is not asking for any child support from Flavie, whether or not she actually begins working.

and out of free-riding and work legally so that she could properly take care of the two children in Cameroon that she has very unnecessarily prevented me from bringing to Canada through her (see Fossungu, 2015a: 56-57 & 59-65). You can as well realize that this *Requête* of mine greatly, if not totally, inspired the JCA, which, itself, had the additional advantage of permitting me not to quit the out-of-town job to be in town for the alternate weekly show. On reaching that agreement (the JCA), therefore, and also viewing the expenses involved in the unexpected court fight (see Fossungu, 2015a: 69-71), I formally sent my lawyer this "CLOSURE OF FILE PETER FOSSUNGU C. HENRIETTE FLAVIE BAYIHA" letter on February 13, 2013:

Dear Me. Grenier:
I would like to have the abovementioned file with you closed. As you well know, I was never out to spend the kind of money (which I do not even have) that I now owe for your services. If Ms. Bayiha has no responsibilities, I have a lot of them (child support, rents, etc.) and am someone who loves respecting my engagements. Henceforth, if Ms. Bayiha cannot see reason, then she would be the one to go unnecessarily spending money, not me, because I do not know even how I am going to come up with the additional two thousand and sixty-eight dollars for payment of something that was initially so plain and straightforward.

In that regard, I am requesting the settlement of this amount by four monthly payments, the first payment of five hundred dollar (500$) for this month being here included.
Thanks.
Peter A. Fossungu.

Did I predict well? The next chapter will help you to answer by examining the gold-digging enterprise's strategies for reversing from Direction-Windsor to Dolbeau-Forever.

Chapter 2

Battling From Joint Custody To Sole Custody: The Gold-Digging Enterprise Reversing Gear From The University Of Windsor To The Forest University?

When a mother, for instance, is bent on destroying or limiting the partner's chances of progress (solely for her own petty agenda), does she ever realize exactly what she is doing to the children that she is claiming to love, and entitled to full custody of them? Does a mother also have the child at all in mind when she argues unnecessarily with the child's day-care provider? (Fossungu, 2015a: 50-51)

Here we will be studying two phases of the venture, namely, (1) the modified joint custody to introduce children support and (2) the persistent drive to sole custody.

The Shared Custody Plus Children Support (SCPCS): April 2014 To January 2015

This court judgement will be conveniently shortened to the SCPCS. The shared custody agreement (JCA) could not last even a year intact because, from her imbecilic painting of me as a drunkard to secure her facile swim into welfare that has already been largely exposed (see Fossungu, 2015a: 46-73), "Flavie (who loves free-riding a lot) has been doing everything to ensure that I only remain working in the forest. In that way, then, she can easily take cover behind the fact that she has the children anyways, a ploy which also seems to be aimed at furthering her claim to victimhood" (Fossungu, 2015a: 73). Thus, when I got the admission in Windsor the destruction of that Grand Plan was sensed and steps had to be quickly taken to obliterate the option. Otherwise, how do you then explain the following events?

The *Flavischolastical* Property Transfer and *Gravelling* Rambling

Since I was not to be in town and with the children from October 2013 to May 2014 as expected, towards the end of August 2013 I discussed the matter with Flavie in Montreal. I explained to her how (even though I wouldn't be getting as much there as I would, being on employment insurance) the Windsor position was an opportunity that would certainly take me out of the forest-and-away-from-the-children work. Of course, as you know already, that was not something Flavie wanted to see happening. So, she devised every means possible to prevent its materialization, just as she did to the U.S. bar entrance plan (see Fossungu, 2015a: 65). First, she outrightly refused to have my furniture and other useful things to the children, saying they didn't need these things: whereas she and the children were then sleeping on a mere mattress on the floor. At this point I could not help giving Scholastica a lot of *99-sensical* credit. You have just heard above that an important distinction between married (Scholastica) and common law (Flavie) spouses is the right to property when the relationship breaks down. And that couples who live together do not have the same rights as married couples to a share in the value of property, including the home they live in, unless the property is in both of their names. Although married, nothing in the house was in Scholastica's name, except the car I bought for her in her name. That could be the reason she even didn't bother about whether or not the bills and rent were settled, telling me how I alone "will pay these bills until you shit!"

But Scholastica is the very person who boldly asked "for us to share property" when she was ready to move to London, far away from the parasite (me). I just looked at the person seriously talking sharing of property and said: "Since you've made up your mind, without any discussion with me, on taking the kids with you, why don't you also just take whatever property you need?" A very good take-and-take taker, you already know, she is. Professional working-class Scholastica swept everything away with her to London. On the contrary, here was Flavie who has no (sure) source of revenue and to whom I was offering to leave everything she needs. She instead would be telling me she has no need for the things. When I requested dismantling and packing the stuff in her large storage room and paying half of her rents, she would further instead be suggesting her showing me places where storage services are offered! No, No, and No! She said to the offer. Was it something else or this master (or is mistress the right word here?) free-rider was actually refusing to be her true self for *nothing*? The Bangwa have an adage that says you never see the private part of a hen until the wind blows. Was the 'property wind' not blowing here in Montreal?

Flavie's counter storage suggestion quickly reminded me of the hypocrisy in Scholastica's forwarding of a job opportunity for a senior legal officer to me on Tuesday, January 8, 2013 at 11.27 AM to which I had responded on Thursday, January 10, 2013 1:24 PM as follows:

My dear Scholastica:

Thank God I am incapable of hating anyone; and if I could even one day possibly find a little obscure place in my heart for that, it would, for sure, not be for someone I love as much as you. Frankly, if I could harbour hatred in my heart, I would never have grown where I grew, nor even completed primary school. One of the greatest ingredients of my success in life has to do with the fact that I squarely confront the truth about myself as well as about those I deal with. A lot of people (including you) who cannot handle the truth often take my unique approach in life for something else.

Don't you think your hypocrisy and insults to me are going too far? I am referring to your forwarding job vacancies like this one to me. I say this because you know quite well as I do that my professional growth is the last thing (if at all) that you want. Otherwise, first, you would not have told me in 2000 that you could not sponsor me (someone who is almost entirely responsible for making you what you are today) to become a permanent resident and easily get into a professional position. And, second, you would not have tied me up in 2006 with so-called child support at the same time that I was trying so hard to pay back (without even complaining) the debts I had gone into in Cameroon (with Elias Akendung and through Edith-Rosa Khumbah) in order to see you through life. I do not regret at all having done all that and more, and would do it all over again. What I just do not understand is why you have to burn the bridge after crossing the river just to prevent many others from also crossing.

From where, for example, do you expect me to fabricate seven years professional experience today? How do I also cut back my age? I guess you have been so interested in just yourself (and your parents, brothers and sisters) that you cannot even remember my age. I just hope you have already found a suitable 'replacement-father' for our two children in one of their uncles (your brothers). This non-professional man is now fifty-three (53) and soon retiring, with the most important twenty (20) of those 53 years having been sapped away by you, Scholastica, the love of my life. Why?

If you are now interested in seeing me do anything professional until the retirement year hits, then here is what you can do. Give me this 2013 to prepare myself and go and revive the lecturer-in-law position I obtained since October 2001 at the University of Douala. That is the lone way for me now to get back into the professional field; otherwise, just keep sending only your "friendly reminders" in regard of child support to me because I know where and how to go looking for job vacancies that I cannot even apply for. PAF.

Flavie's whole idea then was clearly that I should not be able to have where to leave all those expensive household things bought at The Brick. She knew well that I was obviously not going to dump them in the garbage and leave. The proof is in her asking for these same things in May 2014 when I came up for the court session that she started in September 2013. At that time I merely informed her that these things could be so easily gotten if she could be able to find the passageway to and back from hell. In 2013, I necessarily had to be in Windsor by September 3 to be able to attend the compulsory orientation on the next day. I thus contacted Michel Ndikumana to see if I could share his apartment. He understood my predicament and Rue Ward thus became my new official address in Montreal while I was in Windsor. As usual, I notified Flavie of this address at which I even spent a night with the children before heading to Windsor on September 3, 2013.[32] As the moving to

---

[32] Back again in Montreal, for instance, on Friday March 1, 2015, I duly notified Scholastica of my contact information as follows:

Dear Scholastica: I hope everyone is doing fine over there. Just to let you know I have completed the Windsor programme, having been without a phone or internet connection at home for the last eight or so months. Just happy that it's over and I am now back in Montreal since February 1, 2015. Until something hopefully comes up, I will be at the following address: 20-10410 Terrasse Fleury, Montreal, Quebec H3L 3L4 Canada. My magic jack phone below [in signature line – 514 418 3639] plus 438-381-8451 are now running since yesterday. Extend my greetings to Ngunyi and Nguajong. All the best. Chief Fotale'eh

Windsor could not be hampered, the gear would be shifted by *Flavigravellism* into the reverse one.

Of course, I should normally have been sending money to Flavie from Windsor. But how could that even be when, because of her designs, I had to be paying double (one-and-half) rents and meeting up with other financial obligations from my graduate assistantship of about $1200.00 per month? The position here is tantamount to Scholastica's heartless and hidden-agenda asking for child support arrears in Ontario which led to the write-up in London's Court File N° 1162-05 titled "Child Support Arrears: Give the Respondent a Break" that is fully discussed in chapter 3. Remember that, on reaching Windsor, I also had to contact Scholastica to both notify her of my address and request for a hold on child support payments until I was done with the programme that I was hoping would get me out of the usual position I was in.[33] Scholastica grudgingly understood but not the perpetual free-rider called Flavie.

Realizing that I still made it to Windsor despite her schemes to frustrate my graduating from forest work, just hear what plot Flavie and her lawyer hatched. On September 11, 2013 they went to court lying as usual and demanding children support; having me served at the De Nancy address that they knew well was no longer valid. The idea, you still want me to spell it out? That the court should decide everything in my absence, especially as they feigned complete ignorance of my whereabouts and how to reach me. Good learning from the Master of Child-Support Business School, you want to say

---

[33] Even my friends in Edmonton find it hard to understand my case. For instance, on Thursday, June 14, 2012 12:11 AM Nancy Whistance-Smith stated somewhere in her letter to me: "I have no idea why you are no longer living with Flavie or your two younger children, but whatever the reason, you need to look beyond your (ex)wives and focus on what is best for your children. We remain puzzled that with two Masters Degrees and a Ph.D. you are unable to find employment that pays more than minimum wage."

here? Well, your guess will be as good as mind if you know from chapter 1 above that it was only in the London court house that I realized that divorce even was part of the package, when I was wondering what the basis of the hide-and-seek *Asahchop v. Fossungu* suit was. The *Bahiya* team claimed in the Montreal Court in April 2014 that they didn't have any means of reaching me, which is why they instituted the suit for sole custody and child support. Do liars ever think straight? Are they not intentionally forgetting that on Wednesday April 24, 2013 at 1.39 PM I had sent Mr. Gravel an email? It stated: "Hi: Here is my T4 etc. for 2012. Thanks. Peter." That electronic communication was followed up on Thursday April 25, 2013 with another email: "Hi Maitre Gravel, I have just realized that I forgot to send this document (attached here) in last communication. Thanks. Peter." On Wednesday May 8, 2013 at 4.52 PM I also sent to the lawyer the final London court judgement (attached) with this message: "Hi Maitre Gravel: I received this in the mail yesterday. Thanks. Peter." You can thus see that their claim of ignorance of my contact had a hidden agenda just like Scholastica's case of wanting child support through lies and other fabricated offences.

Unfortunately, for these child support schemers of the Business School, the courts must have realized that I was never actually served in September 2013 by the *bailiff* at the faulty address they had intentionally provided. Hence, on February 13, 2014 the *Bayiha* hijackers had a *Nouvel Avis de Présentation* prepared and sent by registered mail to my Windsor address! How did they now know my whereabouts and full address? Accompanying the September 11, 2013 *Requête de la Partie Défenderesse pour Pension Alimentaire et Garde d'Enfant (Art. 813.9 C.P.C.)*, the *Nouvel Avis* stated that "*PRENEZ AVIS que la présente requête sera présentée à nouveau pour adjudication devant la Cour Supérieure du district de Montréal, siégeant en division de pratique, le 1ᵉʳ avril 2014 à 9 heures, ou aussitôt que conseil pourra être entendu, au*

43

Palais de justice de Montréal, 1 est rue Notre-Dame, en salle 2.17.
VEUILLEZ AGIR EN CONSÉQUENCE"

En agissant en conséquence, on March 9, 2014 I directed my "Request For A Reschedule Of Court Appearance Date For N° 500-04-060196-137," addressed to Me. Patrice Gravel, which read:

Dear Sir,

From March 26 to April 16, 2014 I have Class Presentations, Submissions of Term Papers, and Final Examinations, etc. all tightly lined up. I cannot therefore find a way to be in Court in Montreal on April 2, 2014 without seriously compromising some of them. For example, in one of my courses I am presenting on March 26, 2014, its final paper is due on April 7, 2014 and examination is on April 12, 2014. On April 2, 2014 particularly I also have a class presentation and an *in-class* paper submission in other courses. My current financial situation does not permit my moving around by plane. Windsor is about ten-hour drive from Montreal. That means I have to be in Montreal by March 31, at the least, to be able to attend the court session on April 1, 2014; making it impracticable for me to be in class for a presentation and an *in-class* submission of a term paper during the morning of April 2, 2014.

Also, I am assisting a professor in a course (Comparative Politics) and do have strict deadlines to meet with weekly online discussions, and grading of assignments and examinations; the scripts of final exam in this course will be coming in on April 9, 2014.

Brief, I would like to request a rescheduling of the court date to any time after April 20, 2014. Thank you for your comprehension.

Sincerely,

Peter A. Fossungu

Patrice Gravel would just not get any sleep until he has fooled someone and/or the court into granting his client what they want to accomplish by whatever means. Thus, he responds to my request with a funny request of his own. On Friday, March 14, 2014 10:10:34 AM, he wrote:

> Bonjour Monsieur: Il faudrait que j'obtienne un jugement intérimaire de garde pour Madame, pour ce qui est de la pension alimentaire nous pourrions remettre la requête le 23 ou le 24 avril 2014 à votre convenance. Pourriez-vous me faire parvenir un courriel attestant que vous vous êtes d'accord pour que de façon intérimaire Madame obtienne la garde le 1er avril 2014, puisque de toute façon Madame assume la garde depuis juin 2013, et nous pourrions faire les représentations nécessaires pour la pension alimentaire le 23 ou 24 avril 2014. Vous pourriez me répondre par courriel rapidement s.v.p.
> Patrice Gravel, Avocat, Médiateur.[34]

As the Chapter 3 court-drama also further portrays, in this man's head, from day one, he assumes that, because Flavie abducted those children without any Canadian authority coughing about it, she is entitled by the mere fact that she physically has them, to have the court issue the piece of paper attesting to and legalizing that. To him, nothing else counts except the fact of physically having the children: irrespective of whether or not they eat every day, attend day-care/school, etc. Lawyers indeed! For those who are not attentive, Patrice Gravel is talking of my giving consent that their questionable September 11, 2013 *Requête de la Partie Défenderesse pour Pension Alimentaire et Garde d'Enfant (Art. 813.9 C.P.C.)*, be validated *in*

---

[34] MLT: Essentially, the lawyer is demanding that I speedily visa their scheme with the court – letting Flavie have sole custody of the children with us meeting in court later just to determine the child support amount that I should be paying to her.

the meantime, with us next meeting in court just to determine how much I have to pay as child support. Remember that, composed of seven paragraphs, it demanded sole custody of the named children since, according to them, Flavie is actually the one having "la garde physique des enfants mineurs" (paragraph 4), it being in the children's best interest that sole custody be given to Flavie who "est la partie la plus apte à l'assumer" (paragraph 5). A sure *Marsian* on Venus foolishly passing for a *Venusian*, this man must be. But since the *Venusians* appear not to know what a *Venusian* actually is, why wouldn't the stranger easily pass for a Native: unless a clever *Jupiterian* can help to make them know it? In addition, the *gravelling* liars are asking for child support to be fixed and paid to Flavie according to the law (paragraphs 6 & 7). And the conclusion:

PAR CES MOTIFS, PLAISE AU TRIBUNAL: CONFIER à la partie défenderesse la garde des enfants mineurs…; **FIXER** selon les règles de fixation des pensions alimentaires pour enfants une pension alimentaire pour le bénéfice exclusif des enfants mineurs, le tout payable selon la Loi facilitant le paiement des pensions alimentaires; **ORDONNER** que la pension alimentaire à être versée pour le bénéfice exclusif des enfants mineurs soit indexée suivant la loi; **RÉSERVER** à la partie défenderesse le droit de prendre toute autres conclusions additionnelles, si besoins est; **ORDONNER** aux parties de se conformer au présent jugement; LE TOUT avec dépens. (Paragraphing altered)[35]

Quite apart from what has been protractedly said in the book on overhauling Canadian immigration, employment, and

---

[35] MLT: For the above reasons, it concludes, the Court should issue an order: conferring sole custody of the children to Flavie; fixing the amount of child support Peter has to pay to her, according to the applicable law in place; ordaining that the parties respect the court ruling to the letter, while also reserving to Flavie the right to ask for retrospective payments of the child support amount.

welfare policies (Fossungu, 2015a), on Friday March 14, 2014 at 8.35 PM I wrote back to the *gravelling* tricks as follows:

> Good evening Sir,
>
> I am greatly amused by your talk of your client having full custody of our children. (This could be understandable though to someone who knows you are dealing with a client who does not like telling it as it is.) We had an agreement on shared custody. These children are not going to be raised on welfare as long as I, their father, am still alive and kicking. If you want to know how serious I am about it, consider these supporting facts: why would a doctorate degree holder have been working in the forest for the past four years? Why would a holder of such a degree be back in school pursuing a master's degree? Simple. Anything that would aid me to take care of my children by myself, I will do rather than relying on welfare to do so. I am not there right now simply because I am currently trying to put myself in a position from which I can both provide and be there for them.
>
> But it seems to me that your client (who loves free-riding on others a lot) wants to hide behind my diverse efforts to secure a better future for these children, to claim sole custody of them. I am here saying therefore that only the court will decide if either of us merits having sole custody: after all the evidence from both sides has been provided to it, come 23 or 24 April 2014.
>
> Thank you.
>
> Peter A. Fossungu

Shared Custody Plus Child Support: The April-Fool Decision?

On April 28, 2014, as you already know, Flavie was back in court persistently asking for the sole custody and children support from Peter who had gone to school in Ontario in September 2013. Because this time around Justice Michèle Monast (unlike the others) paid very close attention to what Peter also had to say (as to more of which, see Fossungu, 2015a: 29-31), the court ended up maintaining the shared custody agreement intact while ordering the payment of children support by Peter. That is, children support in addition to also paying day-care for one child. The full judgement is outlined here and would be very useful in chapter 3 where I analyze the other decision that ignorantly repudiates it. The full Monast-Decision (as per the PROCÈS-VERBAL D'AUDIENCE) is as follows:

Vu la requête pour garde et pension alimentaire présentée par la défenderesse,

Vu l'affidavit et les pièces versées au dossier ainsi que les représentations faites par le procureur de la défenderesse et par le demandeur qui se représente seul;

Considérant que la preuve révèle que les enfants... résident avec leur mère qui en assume la garde de fait exclusivement depuis le mois de mai 2013;

Considérant que la preuve révèle que le demandeur réside actuellement à Windsor (Ontario) où il poursuit des études de maitrise et qu'il ne prévoit pas être de retour à Montréal avant le mois de septembre 2014;

Considérant qu'il parait être dans l'intérêt des enfants que le TRIBUNAL se prononce de manière intérimaire sur leur lieu de résidence et sur la pension alimentaire qui doit être étable à leur bénéfice jusqu'en septembre 2014;

PAR CES MOTIFS:

Le TRIBUNAL prononce l'Ordonnance de sauvegarde pour valoir jusqu'au 26 septembre 2014;

ORDONNE que les enfants ... continuent de résider avec leur mère et fixe la pension alimentaire payable à leur bénéfice au montant de 333.33 par mois à compter du présent jugement;

ORDONNE au demandeur de payer ladite pension alimentaire directement à la défenderesse jusqu'à ce que les percepteurs des pensions alimentaires procèdent à l'ouverture du dossier et par la suite conformément à la loi facilitant le paiement de la pensions alimentaire;

Réserve à la défenderesse ses droits et recours pour réclamer un ajustement de pension alimentaire de manière rétroactive, le cas échéant;

Déclare que les droits d'accès auprès des enfants seront exercés selon l'entente à l'amiable entre les parties;

ORDONNE aux parties de se communiquer mutuellement leur déclaration de revenu dans un délai de 15 jours;

Continue les requêtes tant en demande qu'en défense au 24 septembre 2014 en salle 2.17

Le Tout sans frais.[36]

Note also that the children support was not calculated based on half-month – which is normally supposed to be the case in shared custody - but full month. It was all the handiwork of the woman's lawyer. But I had no real problem with that since this judgment was globally the best thing to do

---

[36] MLT: Having considered all the pieces of proofs and other relevant facts of the case, as presented by the parties; noting that the children actually reside with their mother while their father is out-of-town and studying in Windsor, Ontario; being aware that these children's best interests dictate that there be available finances for their upkeep as well as an officially known place of abode for them; this Honourable Court makes the following temporary order which is effective until September 26, 2014 and (1) gives their mother physical custody of them, with the absent father paying child support for their benefit, during that period, in the monthly amount of $333.33 directly to the mother until the Family Responsibility Office has duly created an account for the purpose, (2) preserves the mother's right to request for retrospective child support, if need be, and (3) access rights are to be arranged by the parties who must also mutually communicate their financial situations within two weeks; with the next hearing being fixed for September 24, 2014 in Room 2.17 of the Courthouse.

for the children following my desire to graduate from the forest university for good, a yearning hinged on my impassioned plea to "the [Monast] Court to tell me anything other than that it was letting Flavie have full custody of the children that she is merely using for her schemes. No matter how much I disagree with her free-riding comportment, I have never intended keeping her away from our children. Also, my paying child support is not the issue; it is the question of what is best for the children."[37] And continued shared custody was that best option, in my view. And there is much evidence to attest to the position.

Child support is a common requirement and is paid by the noncustodial parent to the custodial parent as assistance in raising the child. The typical arrangement is subject to exceptions because some American states allow parents to retain joint physical custody, in which the child spends equal time with both parents. For example, in California the Family Code establishes a presumption that joint custody is in the child's best interest, thus placing joint custody as a preferred option when courts make custody determination in that state.[38] Advocates of joint custody argue that it lessens the feeling of losing a parent that children may experience after a divorce, and it is fair to both parents. Many courts, on the other hand, resist ordering joint custody if either parent does not want it, due to the high degree of cooperation it requires, especially when the children involved are young or if the parents live a

---

[37] Fossungu, 2015a: 33. Of course, the Monast verdict was long anticipated; explaining why my Leave of Absence Application to the University of Windsor is dated April 8, 2014. In it my 'Reasons for Leave of Absence' were "(1) DON'T HAVE THE FINANCIAL RESOURCES (2) NEED TO SPEND TIME WITH MY CHILDREN AND SETTLE SOME FAMILY ISSUES (SEE ATTACHED DOCUMENT)." The attached document is the April court appearance notification.

[38] See California Family Code Annotated § 3040 (West 1995).

great distance apart, such as in separate states.[39] In *Henriflavipeterism* there was already shared custody plus child support from the temporarily-away parent and it was understood that he would be returning soon from Windsor to Montreal.

From Windsor To Dolbeau-Mistassini, Never To Montreal: *Tremblaybullshitation* And Extreme Gold-Digging

Not so with the other side that was bent on reversing Windsor, as you can see in the effects of the April 2014 decision: From Windsor to Dolbeau-Mistassini, never to Montreal. You would grasp the momentous effect of the decision if you have a bit of knowledge of what my Windsor plans consisted of. I can write a whole book on that. But let me cut it short with acquainting you with just my "MA Internship System Statement of Intent" that was submitted as part of the admission application for the programme. It read:

I am interested in an internship as part of my MA in Political Science program for a number of reasons, the most crucial of which follows. I am in this program of studies principally because I intend to effect some political changes to society in Africa notably, drawing from my unique experiences in Canada. I am certain that an internship in a Canadian political institution as part of my University of Windsor MA degree will evidently help me to understand and grasp the strategies required to better accomplish my goals, since it will mean my being able to synchronize or blend (something I like to always do: see my 2013 *Africans in Canada: Blending Canadian and African Lifestyles?*) the theory and practice of political science. In

---

[39] http://legal-dictionary.thefreedictionary.com/Child+Custody

other words, make political science relevant to real life, to real people in the real world. Is there any better way, for someone with my objective, to go about it?

That therefore explains not only why I am requesting selection for the internship but also why I am in this MA program in the first place. A brief résumé is attached.

Thank you.

Sincerely,

Peter A. Fossungu

Leaving the Montreal court in April 2014, I had to let go of that objective since pursuing it further would have been inviting the same situation and problems that had befallen me with the London case after I lost my job – garnishee orders from Justice Canada, left and right, up and down, inside and outside. I just had to request not only being dropped out of the Internship stream but also took leave of absence from the programme and the consequent assistantship and returned to work in Dolbeau-Mistassini from May to September 2014. It was a wise decision because, added to all the court and child support headaches, my mother's illness and death came knocking and would necessitate my travelling to Africa twice (May & July 2014). The internship stream is also a better way to secure a job after the course. I called off all of that in order to avoid the child support and other troubles. But did I actually stay clear of same? How could I ever do so when compulsive gold-diggers and *tremblayingbullshitters* are over the place to see me down?

Since the April 2014 decision, I have had to go through hell (especially on my return to Windsor to complete the voluntarily cut-off programme). You get a glimpse of what I mean to say from a few communications with/to people who have been complaining of this and that regarding my 'changed lifestyle'. For instance, to Paul Ayah who had sent a message requiring my calling him for some discussions, I wrote this email on

Friday, November 14, 2014 at 1.32 PM: "Hi Paul: I got your message. It is not feasible for me to call since I do not have internet at home or any other phone. It is not possible to use a calling card with the public phones here, I do not know why. I have tried doing so several times and the option does not go through. Right now I am going through hell here since I never foresaw still being here [in Windsor] at this time: all thanks to Flavie and her court issue. But I am hopeful that everything will soon work out just fine. Extend greetings to the family. Peter " On Sunday, November 30, 2014 at 7.42 PM my similar response to the email of the Fon of Nwangong was:

His Royal Majesty:

Thank you very much. It is practically very difficult for me to call anyone right now since I don't have a phone now and in this city I am in now I have no friends at whose homes I can make the call using a calling card. It is because of this problem that I have not been able to communicate by phone with anyone since I got here in October. I easily get information sent through fossungupa@yahoo.ca (which I consult daily) than through this particular email which is often flooded with group postings. Please use but that email for future communication. Right now I have calling cards that I cannot use because the public phones here in Ontario do not permit my going through the process. I may be defending this December, if all goes well and will then be returning to Quebec. Even my daughter, Kelie, cannot understand why I have not called her since returning from Cameroon but I can only do what I can do when I can do it.

Extend greetings.

Dr. Peter Ateh-Afac Fossungu

Imagine going through all this hardship just to make sure that you provide for your children, as per a court order which you did not even need,[40] only to be caused to be branded as a defaulter by back-stabbers. I am a very patient and calm person. But I really would be lying like Flavie if I say that I have much patience and composure with backstabbers and schemers like Flavie. Let me prepare you for 'The Family Backstabbing Show' with a Canadian financial institution, since we are here talking Money-Only matters. On March 20, 2015 I

---

[40] That I hate feeling like it is because of a court order that I am providing for my children, can be discerned from the fact that I have never been interested in asking for child support, were I to be granted sole custody (see Fossungu, 2015a: 30). It is also seen from this Agreement I entered into on December 21, 2010 in order especially to sponsor the same woman (Flavie and children tied to her) who is today trying to plunge me back into that horrible well. Opening with "Dear Scholastica" the Agreement read:

In order to take the matter out of the hands of those who do not know this family as well as you and I, I am proposing this Agreement between you and I regarding child support for the period I was out of work and unemployed:

1. You, Scholastica Achankeng Asahchop, agree to unilaterally withdraw, as Recipient, the Child Support Order from the Family Responsibility Office (FRO) in order to permit me, Peter Ateh-Afac Fossungu, to be able to pursue my daily activities without all the hindrances emanating from that Office, and without this awkward feeling that I am being forced to take care of my own children.

2. I, Peter Ateh-Afac Fossungu, agree to pay to you, Scholastica Achankeng Asahchop, a total of seven thousand dollars (7000.00$) as arrears for the said period (as of today the Fonds des pensions alimentaires puts it at eleven thousand two hundred sixty-eight dollars – 11,268.00), payable in monthly amounts of at least two hundred dollars (200.00$), commencing from date of effective end of the FRO intervention till the entire amount is paid off.

3. Regular monthly payment of child support of four hundred and twenty-eight dollars (428.00$) continues as usual, with or without this agreement.

4. With this Agreement applying therefore you should be receiving directly from me at least six hundred twenty-eight dollars (628.00$) per month in two lump sums (i.e., two different cheques, for easy accounting). The Child Support Order could still be re-registered later with the FRO, if need arises.

Thank you for considering this matter as one that is designed for the interest of especially our children.

Sincerely, Peter Ateh-Afac Fossungu

wrote a "Complaint Against Fraudulent and Malicious Treatment" to TransUnion's Investigation Department (they are based in Hamilton, Ontario), stating:

Dear Sir/Madam:

I am really surprised and angry. Despite my relentless efforts to clean up my messy credit situation in the 2007-2008 period Canadian Tire Bank has long decided to leave an inexplicable stain on my name with a so-called debt that has long been paid. I only discovered this trick on Tuesday 17 March 2015 when I applied for a Royal Bank of Canada credit card. Unlike the others who usually just say "NOT APPROVED," The RBC agent was kind enough to explain the exact problem to me, informing me that "Canadian Tire Bank Account 5446120054509044 Showing R9 -> Bad Debt Written off". I just could not believe what I was hearing because that is purely not true. These are the facts:

• In May 2007, I received my last Canadian Tire Bank Credit Card statement that you can find in this complaint. That same month I also received the May letter (Final Notice) from Agence de recouvrement TCR lltée that is also included here.

• On 22 June 2007, I paid $500.00, using the payment stub of the May 2007 statement. Thereafter I received another letter dated 27 June 2007 from Agence de recouvrement TCR lltée (included here) [which reflects the payment].

• On 20 August 2007 (using the April 2007 statement stub), I paid $663.04 with a TD VISA cheque #503. This payment is clearly reflected in TD VISA's September 2007 statement that I have included here.

With these documented facts, therefore, please tell me exactly what the written-off debt is that is on my credit file till date. Why would I have paid off all the other credit cards and other debts except that of Canadian Tire Bank?

Why would Canadian Tire Bank have notified TCR Lltée of the June payment but not also of the August payment? I need this vexing issue on my credit standing resolved as fast as possible.

Sincerely yours,

Peter Ateh-Afac FOSSUNGU

For over a month since I complained, nothing has been done by TransUnion. Imagine that it was Canadian Tire Bank that sent the message to them on me. Of course, my name would instantly have been all over the place with *Red Lights* flashing incessantly. On the contrary, TransUnion seems to have instead transmitted my contact information to its myriad of hawk-like clients/associates. Now, is the Consumer Protection Bureau that all these collection agencies and others keep referring their supposed DEBTORS to, of any aid to the consumer? There is absolutely nothing of the sort, if you ask my view. That bureau is just there to camouflage that the 99% being exploited has some sort of protection against the 1% that has them under chains. Get the *expibasketical* exemplification, also "free of charge," from the *Videotron File*.

Before I left Quebec for Ontario (Windsor) in September 2013, I asked Videotron if they could move my services (phone and internet) to Windsor. They made me to understand it wasn't possible since they do not cover Ontario. I therefore requested discontinuation of the services, indicating that I was happy with their service and that whenever I return to Quebec I would like to stick with them. In February 2015 I called them and got internet and phone service set up at my current 10410 Terrasse Fleury address. On Wednesday, 13 May 2015, I got a letter from a collection agency based in Rimouski (Quebec) claiming that I owe their client (Videotron) $400 plus. I didn't quite understand the contents and called Videotron. Verification indicated that my account with Videotron had zero dollars in red. I then called the collection agency (as per their letter to me) which advised me to call their client again and refer to the reference number on the letter they sent to me. I did that and a Videotron customer service representative checked the file and explained that, true, I had suspended the services in September 2013; but that the $400 plus was charges for services they rendered to me in 2014! He went on to precise that I had promised to reactivate the services in 2014, and concluding that, because I didn't do so, they therefore sent the file to the collection agency.

I effectively cancelled the services as already noted above. But my hard questions to him was: assuming that I only suspended (as you say), as I didn't reactivate in 2014, how come you claim that you did provide me with services, and at which address? If I had really been owing money to Videotron from 2014, how could they have offered me services in February 2015 (a different contract number) if the said contract at Rue De Nancy was then in the red? Note that the first question that these companies ask whenever you request for services is your Social Insurance Number (SIN) that brings up everything about you in their system. To these *fossungupalogistic* queries, that agent's response was simply: "Sir, you have the option to pay the debt or have your credit seriously ruined. You just have to pay the amount owed." I made it crystal clear that I was the wrong person they had chosen for their hoodwinking pranks because I owe them nothing. I then returned to the collection agency's official, as instructed by her. She too also made it clear that I have to just settle the debt in order not to soil my credit rating. I explained everything relating to the *Videotron Joke* to her, making it clear that I was not owing Videotron anything. She just kept intimidating me and harping on the fact that I have to pay, and even going further to offer to "do something" by reducing a few dollars: if I accepted to pay immediately by credit card. My unwavering response was that I was not paying even a dime as a debt that I did not owe to anyone. That only in court would I be made to do anything of the sort. I just had to bang the phone on her ears as she just kept insisting that I have not *proven to her* that I do not owe their client.

Similarly, I closed an electricity account with Hydro Quebec in September 2013 since they too are limited in their business to Quebec. They asked for an address to which to send my final bill. Because I was still to acquire one in Windsor, I gave them the Rue Ward address for the purpose. Michel Ndikumana had my authorization to open all my correspondences, scan them and send to me as email attachments. He did an excellent job. I eventually got the Hydro final bill and sent them a cheque which they duly cashed. Thereafter, they surprisingly continued to send monthly electricity bills in my name to Rue Ward. I then wrote to them inquiring: (1) when I ever requested electricity services from them at the Rue Ward address, (2) when the original occupant (Michel) ever cancelled his electricity contract with them, and (3) whether they can possibly be providing electricity services simultaneously to two different persons at the same address. (Sleeping Canadians had better wake up!) They then wrote to me, apologising for the *mix-up*.

But on May 19, 2015 I received Groupecho Collection's letter (*Avis de Réclamation*) of May 14, 2015 that boldly claims that I am owing their client, Hydro Quebec, the sum of $110.56; and ordaining that "Votre remise pour le montant complet doit être recue à nos bureaux dans les **48 heures** suivant la reception de cet avis." I got this nonsensical letter as I was about to travel to northern Quebec. But I intend to later communicate with its author, Valerie Robichaud, to let her know that they and their *thiefing* client would only forcefully squeeze that sum out of me through the Canadian infamous courts. Now, if you can imagine what they would then have spent in order to steal that amount of money from me, then you would have really understood where I am coming from as well as where I am heading to: because I still have all the relevant documentation intact. These papers would have to be turned over to the Canadian Courts that might then choose to ignore them *à la manière de* Montreal's *Zigzagging-Gravelling* Family Court. To these so-called collection agencies, therefore, I was already a DEBTOR before I had actually become one, *une fois de plus, à la manière de Québec's bureau des pensions alimentaires.*

Lapidationism, *Flavischolarism*, and the Value of Archives: Family Irresponsibility Naked on the Streets

Michel Ndikumana has a real problem with me for refusing to throw away 'outdated stuff', as he puts it. Yeah Michel, you are exactly right and I know you went through hell living with my archives of these and those. I guess I would not have gone through the pains of unnecessarily redoing what I had already done: had Scholastica not been an unscrupulous 'property sweeper'. Yes. You got that correct. Included in what was swept away to London was our home computer that had every research of mine ever recently done till then. I lost all of that (having especially to retype all of what I already had in soft copy) from the hard copies of those few researches that I was lucky to still have in that form. All this happening because, despite her having updated to sophisticated laptops and clearly not needing the old machine, Scholastica would not let me have the old computer that was dumped in her basement (as I demanded in 2007): "until you have paid me some money for it." I was aware of being married to a *99-senser* but never did I know until then that I actually fell so deeply in love with a Money-Only Monster! So, my dear friend, Michel: what would I have done if I never preserved and moved around the whole endless July 1st cycle (that we, non-*real estaters*, are stuck with) with the hard copies? Total disaster! It is better to have had to retype than not to have had what to even retype. I would not want to detain you long on that *Scholaparentism* Planet. But let us specifically see where I would have been standing today to prove my case against Canadian Tire Bank if I had already shredded all those credit card bills because I had already paid them off? With my 'outdated papers' still available, I am keenly waiting to hear what TransUnion has to say (if they ever would say anything at all) before deciding on my next line of action. Oh these Canadian hoodwinking institutions and the public's interest!

Like the Canadian Tire Bank, *Flavischolarism* would also entail drawing cheques for children support on my CIBC (Canadian Imperial Bank of Commerce) bank account and yet be setting the unthinking and trigger-happy Child Support Enforcement Office behind me. Oh these Cameroonian women in Canada! Haven't you already heard of competing *Grands Ambitions* Thieves? It is not a Francophone thing, mark you. Scholastica did the same when (in order not to forget posting them every month) I handed cheques for the first four or so months to her right there in the London court premises before driving back to Montreal. She went ahead and register the issue with the Family (ir)Responsibility Office (FRO or FIO?) without informing them she already had those cheques. Before you know it the FIO (the real & correct acronym) was behind me with garnishee left and right, notwithstanding that I dutifully informed them that the woman already had cheques that she was cashing every month and that I would be sending cheques to them only on the expiry of the covered months. Ending that note to which copies of the cheques were attached was the question "Was I supposed to send cheques to the FRO for the same months?"

As to the FRO's unnecessary telephone threats, I sent a letter to them dated January 23, 2009 indicating that "I just wish to inform you that I got the voicemail you left on my phone last December 2008. I am still on last resort financial assistance as the attached document can show." It is not even like this was the very first time this office of *Family Irresponsibles* was learning of the situation. Their letter of March 13, 2008 had indicated to me that "you owe $2140.00 in unpaid support" and that the FRO "will not pursue more aggressive means of enforcing payment if you enter into and honour a Voluntary Arrears Payment Schedule." It went on to specify that:

If the Family Responsibility Office accepts your proposal, it becomes a binding obligation. **If you do not honour the Voluntary Arrears Payment Schedule, or if you do not respond to this letter, we may then take more aggressive enforcement such as:**

- **Seizing your bank account or assets;**
- **Suspending your passport and other federal licences;**
- **Suspending your driver's licence, and**
- **Taking you to court.**

Please note that you will be charged a $400 administrative fee should we have to take any of the above aggressive enforcement actions against you.

You remain under the ongoing obligation to make support payments and we will continue to take action to collect the support arrears regardless of your response to this letter. This may include: filing a writ of seizure and sale against your property, collecting federal funds owed to you such as income tax returns; notifying the credit bureau of your arrears; or collecting money that you might receive from an inheritance or lottery winnings. Any funds collected by these means will reduce your arrears.... [Bold is original]

They talk of this matter like people just arriving on Earth from Jupiter; as if completely unaware of the facts. Get the ridiculous matter "free of charge" (as Chief Fomengang of Njilap in Nwangong likes to say[41]) from my letter of March 22,

---

41 Chief Fomengang is currently the chairman of the Nwangong Chiefs Conference. I vividly remember him and the interview he granted

2008. Titled "RE: OPPORTUNITY TO ENTER INTO AGREEMENT TO PAY ARREARS," it lengthily theorized to the *Family Irresponsibles*:

Dear Sir/Madam: Thank you for your letter of 13 March 2008. Apart from the opportunity you are according me, I think a few issues need to be corrected or clarified here. First, when I copied this Office and the Court about two months ago with documents showing that I was now on the last-resort financial assistance (Social Assistance) program, it should not be interpreted as an indication of refusal on my part to support my children. Rather, it is only to acquaint those concerned with the reason why, since January 2008, I have not been able to honour this natural and legal right of mine. What I just need is a little more time in my job search. We should therefore be clear on the point that I will honour payment of outstanding arrears as soon as I can start working again. You have my word on that.

I have a problem though with the amount of arrears ($2140.00) indicated in your letter. I do require some details as to how you did arrive at that figure, please. I do believe I have made monthly payments of four hundred and twenty-eight dollars ($428.00) beginning October 2006 and up to December 2007. Photocopies of said cheques are enclosed herewith. Even before 26 September 2006 when the foregoing amount was mutually agreed upon and endorsed by both parties, I had been paying toward supporting the children in the average sum of two hundred and fifty

---

"free of charge" to the press during my mother's funeral ceremony in July 2014 in Nwangong. From the same royal family with my mother, he explained a lot of things concerning Nwangong Fondom and its people, its economy, etc. What really stood out in the dialogue has to do with his "free of charge" preface to every request from the pressman if he could answer/explain this or that question/point.

dollars ($250.00) per month whenever I had not been living with them. Photocopies of some of the cheques paid during such periods are also enclosed, together with a document (that is in the Court's Continuing Record of File # 1162-05) detailing child support cheques drawn by the Recipient on the Payer's bank accounts. Frankly, I do not think I ought to be lumped up with people who would need to be threatened in order for them to take care of their children. But, as I have made it clear time and again, I can only do what I can do when I can do it. I do hope that your Office, unlike the Court before it, can comprehend and not ignore the simple truth which is that, to ameliorate the situation, rather that deteriorate it, Case # 0717008 does not require to be pursued with "more aggressive means of enforcing payment."

As things currently stand, it will simply be fooling both the FRO and myself to say that I can actually honour my regular support payment and *any* Voluntary Arrears Payment Schedule (VAPS) with my present last-resort financial assistance of five hundred and seventy-five dollars ($ 575.33) per month. The last four months have been hellish to me as this amount of money cannot even cover my most basic needs of feeding and accommodation. Winter is hopefully past and one can only expect that job availability here will soon improve. I am nevertheless going to fill out the Financial Statement and send to you soon. As for the proposal regarding my regular support payments and a reasonable and regular amount to be paid towards (what I suppose is to be) a revised and/or clarified arrears, it is at present (unless you want me to lie) beyond my reach: even as I intend to eventually honour my responsibility towards my children as soon as I can get off this Social Assistance Program and be back on my own feet. I am doing my utmost best to be self-sustaining again sooner than later. Thank you for your understanding.

Sincerely,

Peter Ateh-Afac Fossungu

All these explications do not matter to them because it was just clearly none of their "SCREW THE MAN UP" business. Yeah Canada: does children's best interest actually mean their father's worst interest? The irony in all of this is that I would go to a Quebec court to have them order off the arrears problem but would be told that *only* the London court itself can do that. And then the London court would disdainfully tell Quebec lawyers trying to help this poor guy on welfare and using legal aid that they cannot represent me in their Ontario. When the fishy *Asahchop* case began, I engaged the services of Me. Jean-Marc Grenier (of LaSalle) to be able to understand what the hell the "Form 39: Notice of Approaching Dismissal" signed on March 10, 2006 by L. McClintock (clerk of the court) was all about. All that the LaSalle lawyer received from the London court was that "We have to hire an [Ontario] agent to represent us. Are [sic] you agree that we do it?"[42] As for the welfare and child support situation, Me. France Brosseau of Verdun would duly brief you on the incommodious issue. She tried her best to aid me but her best was just not good enough to break the 'across-the-province' restriction. But isn't it justly niggling that all this bullshit is never raised when it comes to enforcing that *same* court's questionable *vogelsangian* child support order? Why? Stand behind the Child-Support Business School professionals, for better and for worse! Simple, it is. The Ontario FRO speedily followed up with all its enumerated courses of action and also transferred the case to Quebec's *Bureau des pensions alimentaires* (to also garnishee provincial funds[43]) without anyone ever talking of the court order being

---

[42] Me. Grenier's Letter of August 6, 2006 to me (with a copy of that court's response to him included).

[43] The Quebec (Sainte-Foy) garnishee notice from Justice Canada is dated May 13, 2009 and talks of "Arrears owing: $8132.00 as of the summons issue date of May 6 2009." Denise Roy was in charge of the

from a London-Ontario court. It's all in the business of screwing up the payer, I guess? It is surely Canada-wide as you return to Quebec's *tremblaybullshitation*.

While still in Windsor I was surprised to receive a letter from André Tremblay of *Service des pensions alimentaires* at my 815 University Avenue address. I was amazed because my official address for all these Quebec departments was still on 2375 Rue Ward in Montreal. But mostly astonished, I was, because of the menacing contents of the letter which was dated December 8, 2014, having as the subject line "Terms of the collection procedure applicable to your obligation of support". In the same envelope also was a copy of another letter of the same date that had been addressed to Aménagement MYR with instructions on deduction of specified amounts every two-week pay period to meet up with my DEBT. The firm instructions to MYR were so long, going on and on and on until "Finally, we wish to remind you that this notice remains in effect until you receive a new deduction notice or the Minister of Revenue releases you from this obligation. You may adjust the amount of the deduction only upon receipt of a new deduction notice from the Minister. You must notify us if you are unable to continue making the deduction because the debtor is no longer employed by you. If such a situation occurs, your obligation to deduct support ends without the need for a release from the Minister."

What a stupid policy that brands people debtors before they have even owed a DEBT, you are saying with me? Remember that Justice Monast's judgment made it clear that I was to pay *directly to the recipient until the pensions alimentaires people have set up account.* So, do these people read and understand court decisions that they are supposedly *vigorously* enforcing? Of

---

Asahchop File with the Direction des pensions alimentaires – Québec and did an excellent job in updating, informing and advising me on the issue; understanding my predicament well enough but being incapable of helping without a new court order to that effect.

course, my response to the Tremblay nonsense was not tardy. Neither was it suppliant as some of them would be expecting from a fearful debtor. It was truly *lapidationizing* and meant to strictly find out whoever employed some of these bureaucrats who formulate Canadian policies, without knowing the meaning of terms they employ? Any savvy schoolboy would know that you cannot be a debtor until you owe money. So, foolish welfare bureaucrats keep off calling people debtors until they are. There is more to it than just that though, as you *fossungupalogize* and *lapidationize* along with me on the *tremblaying cockshit*.

Written on December 14, 2014, my reply was titled "Re: Terms of the Collection Procedure Applicable to My Obligation of Support" and read the red fire out of our supposed debtor into the trigger-happy, sexist, and father-bashing *copyocrat*:

Dear Sir, I refer to your letter of December 8, 2014. Would Canadian institutions never stop amusing me a lot with the manner they operate, especially in regard of scheming women? Once a woman walks up to any of these institutions and say this or that, it becomes the final word. The man simply is guilty and has no say whatever! A woman goes to court and lies about this and that and a court decision is issued in her favour, notwithstanding whatever the man says that contradicts her version. She immediately runs to the Family Responsibility Office (whatever you call it in French) and this office also jumps to acting as if the man is in default. Amazing!

Your office has gone as far as contacting my employer to deduct payment of child support directly from them. What does that mean? Of course, it signifies that I have refused to honour child support payments. The woman's word to you is the truth and final, irrespective of what anyone else might have to say. That means, in effect, that I have to double-pay child support to the same scheming recipient and for the same children, right? As you can see from my bank record included here, and marked with an asterisk in red, this woman has been cashing cheques since the month following the court order (May 2014). So, what was/is the reason for her bringing the matter to your office? And what is the rationale for your office doing what it has done without hearing my side of the story? I have personally seen this show before, with the Ontario FRO.

I have absolutely no problem with paying child support because, unlike those always rushing to court for it, bringing up my children is my responsibility. BUT I DO HAVE A HUGE PROBLEM WITH LIES, AND WITH THE PROPENSITY OF CANADIAN INSTITUTIONS ALWAYS BEHAVING AS IF THEY ARE THERE JUST TO DO THE BIDDING OF SCHEMING WOMEN WHO ARE BENT ON "SCREWING UP" NOT ONLY THE OTHER PARENT BUT ESPECIALLY THE CHILDREN THEY ARE CLAIMING TO LOVE AND TO BE ENTITLED TO HAVE FULL CUSTODY OF. IS IT REALLY LOVE OF THE MONEY OR LOVE OF THE CHILDREN?

By the way, I don't know of "the previous deduction notice" you are talking about. My Quebec address on file remains: 2375 Rue Ward #301, Saint-Laurent, Quebec H4M 1T8.

Thank you.

Peter A. Fossungu

Of course, it is not idle talk when I have been saying that the truth hurts, with a whole lot of people not being able to handle it with the equanimity that those of us who can do exhibit. Mr. Tremblay, like the lot of those working in the Canadian public service, must have found this piece of *fossungupalogy* too much to handle and went Wacko. I say this because, despite all the evidence supplied to André Tremblay, I received not only his other letter of December 29, 2014[44] but also a letter (this time through my Quebec address on Rue

---

[44] With "Subject: Obligation to make support payments to the Minister," it read:

On November 26, 2014, a judgment was rendered by the Superior Court of the district of Montéal, requiring you to make support payments to HENRIETTE FLAVI BAYIHA.

The Minister of Revenue sent you a notice informing you that the *Act to facilitate the payment of support* applies to your situation. This means that you must make support payments, including any arrears owing, to the Minister of Revenue for the benefit of the creditor of support, as required by section 2 of the Act.

On December 17, 2014, the Minister sent you a payment order, which is the collection procedure applicable to your situation. Since that date, you have no longer been authorized to pay support or arrears directly to the creditor. Despite the payment order, you have continued to make payments to HENRIETTE FLAVI BAYIHA, in violation of the Act.

We hereby advise you that, effective as of the date of this letter, any evidence you may submit to the Minister as proof that you have paid support directly to the creditor will no longer be taken into account. Since your legal obligation is to pay support and arrears to the Minister, any amount you remit directly to the creditor cannot be recognized as a means of fulfilling that obligation. Therefore, we trust that you will comply with the payment order that was sent to you.

...

In closing, we wish to remind you that it is **your responsibility to inform us immediately of any change** affecting your file, such as a change of address, a new support order or any other situation that you believe should be communicated to us....

Thank you for your cooperation

Signed

André Tremblay

Service des pensions alimentaires F (Bold is original).

One can see just how much Mr. Tremblay was bent on finding fault where none exists. For instance, he is here accusing me of having paid money to Flavie in December 2014 but he was amazingly completely *ignorant* of moneys I paid to her from May to November 2014. How did he even come about with my paying money in December to Flavie when the December support cheque was only duly paid to his *Bureau* in January 2015 after this particular letter of his? Also, where exactly was the Minister's support order he is talking about (that I never saw) sent: to Montreal or to Windsor? And, finally, when did I ever change my address with them from Montreal to Windsor?

Ward) dated January 19, 2015 from Justice Canada giving me "notice that on January 16, 2015 the Government of Canada was served with a garnishee summons. This summons was served by ... Revenue Quebec – Montreal". When are these institutions ever going to be staffed by competent people who separate their emotions and home problems from their duties to the public? In short, I mean people who can keep a level head while serving the public? *Crisebacologist*, that is. I am just using the Tremblay case to make a point but he is not alone, as you have seen and will still see even judges guilty of the same comportment on the bench. You will better handle the continuing mess after I have duly *lapidationized* it.

Lapidationizing Bastien-Bernadinism and the Bearing of the Burden of an Organization's Administrative Blunders: The Public or the Organization?

Lapidationism is a term that derives from a book publishing encounter I had with LAP LAMBERT Academic Publishing which is based in Saarbrücken, Germany. It all began on Tuesday, October 21, 2014 7:41 AM when its Acquisition Editor (Thomas Miller) sent me an email indicating that

I am writing on behalf of LAP LAMBERT Academic Publishing. Your manuscript has been recommended to us by Richard Dwomoh. LAP LAMBERT Academic Publishing specialises in the publication of high-quality research works; to be specific theses, dissertations and postdoctoral theses from respected institutions worldwide. I am therefore wondering if you may be interested in publishing your work as a printed book. I would be happy to receive a positive feedback from you and to answer any further questions you might have, after reading more about us and the publication process itself in the attached document. I am looking forward to hearing from you at your earliest convenience.

On Wednesday, October 22, 2014 05:37 AM, I responded to the unsolicited email (in view of the reference from my University of Windsor colleague who has already published a book with them[45]):

Thanks a lot for your email. Actually, I have not completed research work I am doing here in Windsor. What I have as manuscript is not a thesis or dissertation as such but other independent research that I have carried out from my experience working in Canadian factories. Although academically written, it is kind of experience-based. The manuscript is titled "Africans and Negative Competition in Canadian Factories: Afro-Chinedian Theories from My Extensive Expibasketism" and is already being reviewed by Langaa Publishing in Bamenda, Cameroon which has so far published four of my books. Well, if you think it could be of interest to LAP, then I could let you review it as well. Thanks. Peter (altered paragraphing)

That same day, interest was manifested and, after a lot of other pestering emails, on November 7, 2014 I sent them a new version of the manuscript that Langaa, for over a month, was still reviewing. On November 9, 2014 LAP had already "assessed your work with great pleasure and confirm our interest in publishing it" and providing "the link below" on which to click "within the next 14 days in order to register as author on our website." Before you know it, on November 10, 2014 I am being told that "Your book project 'Africans and Negative Competition in Canadian Factories' (ISBN 978-3-659-63710-0) will soon undergo a technical verification"! What

---

[45] See Richard Dwomoh. *The UN Security Council and Small Arms Proliferation: Legislating the Illicit Trade in Arms* (Lambert Academic Publishing, 2010).

the hell was going on? Does mere registration on their website as an author mean granting publishing rights? I have done that a lot to publishers to whom I have submitted manuscripts that were never eventually accepted. Why was LAP crossing the bridge before it had actually reached it? What a frightening haste! On November 12, 2014 I sent Thomas Miller a message titled "Discontinuation of Publication Process" which indicated as follows:

Please, kindly discontinue the publication process of the manuscript (AFRICANS AND NEGATIVE COMPETITTION IN CANADIAN FACTORIES: REVAMPING CANADA'S IMMIGRATION, EMPLOYMENT AND WELFARE POLICIES?) that I sent to you. I have just been made to understand that I cannot tender any material that has already been published as part of my *ongoing MRP research which is yet to be accepted and defended toward the MA degree that is yet to be granted*. Please, see footnote 11 of the manuscript.

Thank you for your comprehension.

Peter A. Fossungu

P/S: I will try to redo the first two chapters in the context of some other stuff I have been working on and send to you to see if you could like it.

The next day (November 13) Thomas Miller wrote saying that "I am sorry to hear about your decision but could you be more precise about whether you want to discontinue the publication process or you wish to make some changes in the book content. Thank you for your usual cooperation. Looking forward to hearing from you at the earliest. Best regards" (altered paragraphing). Consider the 'best regards' here as Judas' Last Worst-to-You Kiss because this is where *LAPIDATIONISM* puts on its real *tremblaybullshitting* jacket: since someone else would appear from nowhere and begin the menace. Thus, enter Customer Service with Tatiana Taralunga writing on November 13, 2014 to Dear Peter A. Fossungu and thanking "you for your request that was redirected to me. In order [for us] to [have] a better familiarization of the situation (problem occurred), kindly please let us know who is the copyright owner of the already published material and where it was published. Thank you in advance for your help and explanation."

No matter how much I repeatedly explained to this Customer Service what I had told their Acquisition Editor before he disappeared from the scene, they just kept bugging me with talk of having infringed this and that copyright and other such bullshit. Even going further on November 17 to think that they could easily corner me into a publishing undertaking with them when they stated that:

We are thankful for your message although [it] is not a complete one.

As we mentioned in our previous email, the withdrawal of the book from sale leads to enormous costs for the publisher which we will only bear if you will publish your work with us (after defending it). Thus, we would kindly ask you to refer one more time to the above mentioned condition and insure us that you accept the commitment and fulfill it afterwards. Thank you in advance for your collaboration. Looking forward to hearing back from you.

These guys had certainly bitten more than they could chew and, since *fossungupalogy* never sleeps in me, I just had to bring it out full scale to their attention that they weren't dealing with the fool they, until then, thought was under their spell – the DEBTOR, as the Canadian *Family Irresponsables* call it – through this *fossungupalogistic* and *lapidationing* letter of November 18, 2014 01:10 AM:

Dear Thomas Miller & Customer Service:
I gave you the benefit of doubt with the English language when I thanked you for waiving this or that fee,

because there was indeed nothing to be waiving in the first place: if you understand simple English. This leads me to wonder if you even understand the manuscript, written in more complex English, that you accepted to publish.

I told Thomas Miller, when he first contacted me (indicating that Richard Dwomoh recommended me), that my manuscripts were already submitted to Langaa which has already published four of my books. Now, I decided **freely** to submit one of those manuscripts to you, knowing full well that Langaa does not allow multiple submissions. I informed them of my submission to LAP, which meant no further consideration of that particular manuscript by them. That was the end of the matter and I got no childish talk from Langaa as I am now getting from you people of LAP. Let me reiterate it: I remain always **free** to submit my manuscripts when they are ready for submission to **whoever** I decide to submit them to. No one can take away that right from me, both as an individual and as an author/writer. Period!

Perhaps, you ought to make it a main condition for submitting anything to your company **only** in the German language that you are here letting me know is the only language you seem to be able to master. Now, if you will excuse me, I have important things to do with my time than be arguing over very simple and clear English.

Thank you.

Peter A Fossungu [bold is original]

Anyone who never believed in the trunk-cutting powers of *fossungupalogy* as elaborated on in *The HISOFE Dictionary of Midnight Politics* (Fossungu, 2015c) had better see it again here and believe. On Wednesday, November 19, 2014 at 8.25 AM I received this email message from the until-then-threatening Customer Service:

Dear Dr. Peter A. Fossungu,

Thank you for your message.

We are really sorry for the inconvenience. Also we are sorry for the lack of business communication professionalism from your side and the tone of your last message.

I clearly understand that it was a misunderstanding generated of the fact that we work, not only in different departments, but also from different countries with Mr. Thomas Miller. That's why I wasn't aware of your prepublication communication and agreement regarding the Langaa publication. Now as I know that there wasn't any copyright infringement from your side, I would kindly like to ask you to accept my apologies.

Please be informed that your book will be withdrawn from the market within 1- 3 weeks. The withdrawal automatically results in a termination of the contract and your full reclaim of copyrights. Copyrights of the publication and dissemination of your book that passed to our company by accepting our Publishing Agreement on 2014-11-10.

We are sorry that our collaboration ends at this early stage. Nevertheless, we wish you many successful publications in the future.

In case you have any other questions, please do not hesitate to contact me.

Sorry indeed! Did they need the lapidationing letter to really bring them to their senses? And what about the child support office too? Enter Bastienism. I received a letter dated July 16, 2014 (sent to my Windsor address) from Jessica Lafond Bastien of Services des pensions alimentaires B. It was during one of those short breaks from Aménagement MYR at the end of July and, normally, I wasn't supposed to be travelling all the way to Windsor for a three-day break. But I did, just knowing that my address on file with the University of Windsor remained that of Windsor. The Bastien letter indicated that:

We recently tried to contact you, without success, in order to obtain information concerning your file with respect to the Act to facilitate the payment of support.

Upon receipt of this letter, please get in touch with the undersigned at 514 858-3550 (extension 8582482), or at 1 800 545-6486 (extension 8582482) if you are outside the calling area. Be sure to inform this person of your telephone number.

Thank you for your cooperation

Jessica Lafond Bastien

Services des pensions alimentaires B

I could not call during the weekend that was all spent on the road. Back in the Forest World of MYR, I had to lose three days of work, remaining in the camp just to be able to get in touch with Jessica Lafond Bastien but always being received only by her voicemail. Every time I left a message indicating the day I was going to call again. I expressed surprise that I was not sure what information was needed from me and even why the support file was then with them when the support recipient was actually receiving the child support every month – the main reason why I was not even in town but locked up in the forest. That I did not have a phone number at the time through which I could be reached because there is no network in the forest, and how the camp phone that I was using only makes calls, not receives them. I also made it clear that I was there working for Aménagement MYR in Dolbeau-Mistassini and that my official address still remained that on Rue Ward in Montreal, etc. So, if this information is not shared with whoever takes over the file from Ms. Lafond Bastien, what am I to do about that? If you say actually that Mr. Tremblay didn't have this information, then you might also have to prove how he got to know that I was working with MYR to which he quickly sent his support deduction instructions. Or, has the public agent the right to select what information to have and what to feign ignorance of? Brief, is it my business to find out whether or not information I sent to a government department is shared within the department's various divisions? What about taking over a file without knowing whether or not the file you are assuming responsibility for is in order? Enter *Bernadinism*!

Bernadinism: It is not to say though that all workers in the public service are bad. It is just that *na one wow-wow coco di spoil fufu*, is a rule that can hardly be ignored. You get what point I am mustering all my aging force to be able to make from the New Handler of the badly stained File Number 9-00559021-1, alias Superior Court number 500-04-060196-137. I realized on March 10, 2015 that my employment insurance (EI) payment too had been garnisheed for child support arrears. I called the child support section of Revenue Quebec to know why this could be when I was up-to-date with payments. I was expecting to talk to André Tremblay who has never returned my calls. But then I realized it was a different person who was then responsible for the file. After listening to me and going through the file, the new man (Herdeley Bernadin) was really surprised that the matter even had to go to Justice Canada. I had suspected foul play as soon as the first customer service agent I talked to talked of my having two files for the same issue! How could that be, Revenue Quebec? Is that not pure exhibition of malice in public service? Or, more precisely, shouldn't André Tremblay explain that to us and to his employer? That is exactly why I insisted on talking to the one who was in charge of the double-one file: one being in red, red wine while the other was overflowing with juicy excesses (from both garnisheed funds and my regular monthly cheques). WONDER SHALL SURELY NEVER END IN JE ME SOUVIENS QUEBEC (in Hypocratic Canada)?

Herdeley Bernadin explained to me that he had just recently been given responsibility for my file. And he could not stop thanking me for having called because, without the call, he would hardly have discovered the problem. Wasn't he here under-describing the issue? He agreed but begged and assured me that he would do his best to clear the mess. That I should call again in about two weeks to ascertain that everything had already been put on the right track. The last time I called and was transferred to him, it was his answering machine that received me. I left him a message requesting him to call me back since I wanted to have a clear update on the file. I did not immediately get that call but my following IE payments had been made in full and I considered that as proof that the *tremblaybullshitting* has been cleaned up, fortified by Bernadin's call in early April 2015. But it is not so with the court and immigration messes from the gold-diggers and other *tremblaybullshitting* versions.

Chapter 3

Puzzling Judicial And Immigration Family Politics: The March-August Long Night Of The Long-Drawn Swords Against Children's Best Interest?

[H]omosexuality has been legalized in this country that would be claiming multiculturalism but regards polygamy as one of the worst crimes on earth. I know many children of African Muslims who are going through hell here in Montreal because their own mothers could not be here with them since their father is only allowed to be here with only one of his four or so wives. Yet, Canada sees nothing wrong with that; instead preferring to even legalize homosexuals' RIGHT TO ADOPT CHILDREN! I have nothing against these gays and lesbians. But I am not afraid to ask the fundamental questions many are shying away from posing: WHERE WOULD THESE CHILDREN (including the Homosexuals themselves) COME FROM (for them to adopt) IF EVERY ONE ELSE WAS LIKE THE HOMOSEXUALS? Why has the COPYOCRACY refused this time to DO THE COPYING FROM AMERICA? If HOMOSEXUALITY HAS BECOME PART OF MULTICULTURALISM, then WHAT IS THERE TO LOGICALLY KEEP POLYGAMY OUT OF MULTICULTURALISM? Isn't that just part of the Hypocrisy called multicultural Canada? (Fossungu, 2015a: 161).

This chapter has two main parts. The first focuses on the zigzagged case and the manner the modified shared custody judgment (SCPCS) was repudiated in a veiled attempt to ensure that the original joint custody agreement (JCA) would never be restored; while the second handles the effects of parental and institutional errors on children, especially highlighted by cases

79

drawn from the courts and Citizenship and Immigration Canada (CIC).

Zigzagging A Case: The Repudiation Of The SCPCS And The All-Out Stop-JCA Mechanisms

In answering the question relating to how a judge decides custody of, or access to, a child, the Attorney-General of Canada indicates that

Both the *Children's Law Reform Act* and the *Divorce Act* say that decisions about child custody and access are based on the best interests of the child. Factors taken into consideration include:

- The ability of each parent to care for the child
- The ties between the child and each parent
- The stability of the child's current living arrangements
- The strength of each parent's plan to care for the child in the future, and,
- The child's wishes (in appropriate circumstances).

The law also states that the judge must consider violence or abuse when assessing a person's ability to parent.[46]

It must be noted that family law is a federal domain in Canada (unlike in the United States[47]), making province to province variations unnoticeable. With that knowledge in mind, the important question to answer concerns whether or not

---

[46]   http://www.attorneygeneral.jus.gov.on.ca/english/justice-ont/family_law.asp

[47] District and state courts base their decisions on state laws, which may vary greatly among states. If a case challenges the constitutionality of a state law – in rare instances – a state's jurisdiction (that is, its right to decide the case), then the U.S. Supreme Court may issue an opinion. See http://legal- dictionary.thefreedictionary.com/Child+Custody See also Fossungu, 2015b: 195-199.

Justice Jerry Zigman of the Montreal Family High Court took the above listed factors into consideration when he handed down his disturbing judgement that:

For the reason given in presence of the parties and recorded, the Court:

Grants the mother HENRIETTE-FLAVI BAYIHA sole custody of the minor children Peter Jr. and Peteraf;

Access rights for the father Peter Fossungu will be determined amicably between the parties; the court will use the figure of 22888$ as Mr. Fossungu's revenue of 2015, this figure comes from him. The court takes also in consideration that Mr. Fossungu is paying child support in amount of 650$ per month for two children in Ontario;

ORDERS Mr Fossungu to continue paying 333.33$ per month for the two minor children.

In addition, the court ORDERS Mr. Fossungu to continue paying les frais de garderie daycare costs in amount of 158.16$ for Peter Jr. directly to the garderie; the whole without cost.

What a First World court decision! Truly meant for the Hall of Shame, isn't it? The important question any one, lawyer or not, would be sanely asking is: what was actually the reason for Flavie's persistent demand for sole custody? What was actually so wrong in the SCPCS decision that she and her lawyer so badly wanted it gone at all costs? And was the judge who did their bidding here even remotely aware of the decision that he was there nullifying? You get a better handle on these questions and more if you revisit and read that decision of Judge Monast in here again. You know already that, while I was in Windsor to find a way out of the forest, child support was added to the shared custody agreement without calculating the support for half but full month. Being the gold-diggers that some of these African ladies in Canada are, Flavie was still not satisfied and (*à la Scholastica*) went back to the court in January 2015 demanding full custody of the children and children support. At that point, I also made (revived) my own claim for full custody of the children without still asking for any court-ordered children support from my ex-partner. The verdict of the case was set for March 6, 2015, date at which I must have completed my schooling and possibly returned to Montreal.

Justice Monast's April judgement (outlined in the last chapter) was thus not foolish in being provisional until September 2014. That was the normal time I should have completed my programme and returned to Montreal at which time the SCPCS was to certainly fall back into the original JCA with no child support on either side. That occurrence was just not good at all to the *gravelling* gold-diggers and every means must therefore be fashioned to put out that possibility. Hence, the persistent move to get to sole custody decision before the "unproven drunkard-abuser" gets back to town. It commenced earlier but let us begin here with Wednesday October 1, 2014 at 6.18 PM when Patrice Gravel wrote: "Bonjour Monsieur Fossungu, Le jugement intérimaire du 24 avril dernier a été reconduit au 26 novembre 2014, pourriez-vous me confirmer votre présence pour le 26 novembre 2014 en salle 2.17 où votre absence. Patrice Gravel." My reply to the lawyer then followed on Thursday October 2, 2014 at 2.35 PM: "Me. Gravel: Right now I do not know my program for November because I just arrived in Windsor yesterday. But I would be informing you by mid-month; failing which, the present judgement could be extended to January 2015 by which time I am sure I would have left Windsor. Your last email I only got on 29 September 2014 when I reached Montreal because I had been in an area without network. Thanks. PAF" On Friday October 17, 2014 at 3.09 PM I informed Gravel that I would not be able to be in Montreal on November 26, 2014. On Monday, October 20, 2014 5:33 PM, the lawyer wrote, asking for me to choose one of the two dates of 12 or 28 January

2015. And I responded on Monday October 20, 2014 6.43 PM, saying that "28 January could be good. Thanks. Peter." The device for thwarting justice from being done to the children worked well, being assisted by the funny politics of the Quebec family court itself. For instance, take the unwarranted inflation of justices.

The Inflation of Justices: Maybe I Really Don't Know Quebec's Civil Law?

Why was the January hearing not still before Judge Monast but some other justice who merely fixed another hearing date? What was the need for me to come all the way from Windsor to the Montreal court that January 28, 2015? The argument was that it was because I had made my own demand for custody that the scheduling of the March 6 date was necessary. Oh, Quebec's Gang of Liars! So, you can see that, to them, I was just supposed to appear in January 2015 and *kowtow* to what the woman and her Liar had cooked up. Simple as that, isn't it? As you can then see, despite my strong arguments to the contrary, on March 6, 2015 the court (mechanically, you would say?) accorded full custody of the children to Flavie, giving me very uncertain access rights and ordering me to pay a lawyer-only-re-assessed children support based on an imaginary annual earning (remember that I had just left school and still unemployed and job-hunting at the date of the hearing). This same court order went on to mandate that I am still to continue paying one of the children's day-care! What do you call this: Split-Sole-Custody? Only in a Quebec court! There is more and more and more and more. I cannot actually discuss all the imponderables of this court's very faulty litigation politics because I am largely leaving you to answer the Hall of Shame query – my job being mostly to furnish the facts you need for the answering. You just have to review the facts and the decision and continue from there. It seems to be a complete joke that is utterly contrary to children's best interest. But take a few other examples.

If I appeared in the Montreal court thirty times for this same suit, it was before thirty different judges, with most of them consequently not even knowing what the file before them consisted of, and having therefore to rely totally on what the lawyer for the woman was telling them: since most of them (including the lawyer) did not see a black man like me being able to comprehend the niceties of their doings, let alone be of any good. Apart from Justice Michèle Monast who handed down the April 2014 SCPCS verdict, none of these justices ever paid much attention to whatever I had to say. The one between Judge Monast and Judge Zigman (in January) proved to be able to curb Mr. Gravel's very *unlawyerly* court comportment. Take the lawyer's domineering manner of walking at will to my side of the bench and grabbing some documents that I was trying to hand to the court. As the judge said he did not need these documents then and that I should present them on judgment day (March 6, 2015), I requested the lawyer to kindly return the third copy (meant for the other side) that he had snatched. Gravel was not willing to do so, saying the package contained financial documents that he so badly needed. I then turned to the judge to order for the return of my documents and this *lawyer* was still behaving as if everyone else was in *his* court house. The judge was not amused at all when she warned: "YOU HEARD ME RIGHT AND I DON'T WANT TO REPEAT MYSELF, MAITRE GRAVEL!" You will expect that this particular judge will be the one to receive and examine those documents as advised and promised, but she only fixed the new March date of hearing and disappeared. Enter the zigzagging man-machine.

The advocate's *unlawyerlyness* was particularly the case with Judge Zigman who openly confessed that he had no idea what the case before him was all about. He therefore asked the parties to take 15 minutes recess in order to come to an agreement while he (judge) was acquainting himself with the file. Quebec brand of justice, eh? I made it clear to the judge that the suggestion to the parties wasn't necessary since it was because of our inability to agree on very simple things that we were before the judge that morning. That was a statement of fact, if you recall all the phases that this case had passed through to be there that morning. It would appear that Judge Zigman was not happy with this bitter truth (*fossungupalogy*) of mine and became very hostile towards me; behaving as if he (judge) was not aware that, representing myself as I was doing, I had the right to freely object to lies and other irrelevant stuff from the other side's unruly lawyer. For example, you have heard this judge in the judgement saying that my 2015 revenue figure used in determining the two-headed children support was provided by "Peter himself". Not true at all. How would I have been providing revenue for the year that I have not actually worked? The truth is that Flavie's lawyer had already made his calculations based on my 2014 yearly revenue of twenty-eight thousand and something and I merely indicated that the lawyer should be sensible not to forget that I have finished with the University of Windsor. The lawyer immediately jumped to saying that he was taking off what I made last year in Windsor and provided the figure the judge talked about in his judgement. Were they not here pinning me forever to their desired everlasting place of work (the forest in Dolbeau-Mistassini)?

In fact, Flavie's lawyer was actually the judge here and a party. He comported himself in a manner that pointed clearly to the fact that the court was there that morning (as in many of the sessions) just to determine the amount of child support that I was to pay to Flavie (whether or not the supposed payer has a job); and not that the court was there to determine which of the parties was more suited to secure the best interests of the children. Thus, while I had the floor and was explaining how I have returned to Montreal, Gravel cut in at will to incessantly harp that "Monsieur travaille dans le bois à Dolbeau-Mistassini" and how "C'est Madam qui est tourjours avec les enfants." But lies are never consistent; for, is that fact not the reason behind the JCA-SCPCS that they were then seeking to end? Is this not the question that Judge Monast (if still the one hearing the case) would have posed, in view of discovering what changed conditions then necessitated the drive to sole custody? On the contrary and because of the 'justices-inflation', that inconsistent *gravelling* Dolbeau-working reason, of course, is the one and only reason the judge has mentioned in his one-reason-based decision. Read it again! "For the *reason* given in presence of the parties and recorded,..." Nothing in the file of the case mattered at all.

This Quebec *Zigzagging* decision reminds me much about the *Vogelsangian* one in London when Scholastica also ran back to court in 2007 to have an increase in the amount of child support based on the fact I was making more money and "building houses in Cameroon". Despite clear indication to the court that at that moment I was even unemployed and requiring Scholastica to prove her allegations, Justice Henry Vogelsang's Endorsement did the woman's bidding because "Mr. Fossungu did not update his financial information and statement before the trial and thereby breached r. 13(12) of the *Family Law Rules*, O. Reg 114/99. He did not correct his incomplete financial information as required by r. 13(15). I exercise my discretion under r. 13(17)(e) and impute income for 2006 to Mr. Fossungu in the same amount as his assessed income of $41,473 in 2005. If his actual income was, in fact, less than this figure, only he had the proof available, and he failed to put it forward."[48] I humbly submit that judge Vogelsang erred enormously here and this being tied to what I am castigating as the inflation of justices and the disregard of

---

[48] Justice Henry Vogelsang's Endorsement of March 20, 2006, paragraph 5.

information in the court file by those making decisions on the case.

Right now I need only point out, first, that the sacrosanct principle that 'S/he that alleges has to prove' seems to have no home in Anglo-Saxon Ontario, I guess? I returned to Montreal and sent the court (by fax) updates on my 2006 finances with a letter (RE: FINANCIAL/EMPLOYMENT INFORMATION UPDATE) that argued in the first paragraph to "Your Honour" as follows:

It is, and has always been, my belief that the Court can only properly do its heralded job of doing justice to all the parties to any case if, and only if, it has most, if not all, of the essential facts before it. From some of the questions that Your Honour posed to me yesterday (16 March 2007) regarding my financial situation since 2006, I realized that I did not come to Court with some essential documentation. It was simply an honest omission based on two or three interconnected facts. First, the Applicant appears to be doubting the authenticity of the documents (e.g., from Canada Custom and Revenue Agency) that I had filed with the Court. Second, in one of the documents in the Continuing Record I had duly given the Applicant my approval and authorization to obtain directly from the said Revenue Agency whatever financial documentation of mine that she desires. Third, since the only real issue of difference between both Applicant and Respondent turned on the amount of child support payment, I was in Court yesterday solely to learn about the new financial information that the Applicant might have obtained from Revenue Canada (or any other Canadian Government Agency) that I had not been aware of: since the note I got from the Court on 15 January 200[7] (on arriving late due to the snow storm) talked of the Applicant coming back yesterday (16 March 2007) with my 2005 Income Tax

87

Return which was to entitle her to an increased amount of child support, if it showed that I made more than $41,000. Nothing other than the same financial documents already in the Continuing Record (my 2003-2005 income tax returns) w[as] presented by the Applicant.

With all that information and explanation sent to him, the judge had only the satisfaction of the Applicant in his entire head as he went on three days later to order that:

Effective October 1, 2004, Mr Fossungu will pay child support in the monthly amount of $314, based on his 2004 disclosed income of $22,357. Commencing January 1, 2005, he will pay monthly support of $589, based on an income of $41,473. Payments will continue at that rate to and including April 1, 2006. At May 1, 2006, the new tables for the *Federal Child Support Guidelines* increased the amounts payable. See SOR/2005 – 400. From and including that date, Mr. Fossungu will pay the monthly amount of $626 on an income, again, of $41,473.[49]

When I talk of mechanical and father-biased Canadian courts you might think I am crazy or that it is because I am the payer. Think what you may but you can see that Judge Vogelsang had already bought into the woman's lies to an extent that he was just no longer a third-party. You get this sense also from his employment of "his 2004 disclosed income," meaning that I had an undisclosed income – exactly what the woman's whole return to court was all about. Again, was this judge even remotely aware of how the contested $428 per month children support amount that he was then repudiating had been arrived at? He either clearly was not conversant or was but had fervently decided to simply

---

[49] *Id.*, paragraph 6.

"exercise my discretion" to screw up this payer. Otherwise, how come the judge "imputed" the $41,473 as my 2006 income but still went ahead to act as if the imputed amount was higher than what was already there as my 2005 income? Oh! I now see the *Vogelsangian* mathematics! $41,473 in 2006 is greater than $41,473 in 2005 because 2006 is bigger than 2005, isn't it? Are Canadian Family Court Judges not actually true partners-in-crime to the Child-Support Business Scholars? The questions are apt because Judge Vogelsang made that decision notwithstanding that the letter I faxed to him next day after leaving the court unmistakably stated:

Regarding my financial situation since 2006 which, from Your Honour's questioning of yesterday I have now realized, is important to the Court in making a proper and just ruling, I am therefore faxing together with this letter the following documents:

1) My 2006 T4 Slips from:

(a) Dollarama L.P./S.E.C. (showing an annual employment income of $16,205.43),

(b) Premiere Personnel (showing an annual employment income of $17,921.65), and

(c) Randstad Interim Inc. (showing an annual employment income of 4,291.39).

This puts my total employment income for 2006 at **$38,418.47.** (The numerous trips to 80 Dundas Street, London, Ontario, in 2006 did not only affect my annual income but are responsible - though it is not so clearly said - for my loss of employment with long-standing employers.)

If Mr. Justice Vogelsang had read and studied the file as he should have, he would have been aware that the support amount of $428 monthly was arrived at during the Settlement Conference based on the average of my fluctuating yearly income(s) of 2003-2005. There is much to be said about the judge's verdict but let me also highlight the fact that he actually handed to the Applicant in a unique way the same (or even more than) child support arrears that had provoked this reaction and counter-claim from the Respondent that is so important to grasping the points that I need to set it out entirely:

When the Applicant talks of the Respondent paying Child support arrears, a number of questions inevitably crop up. For example, are these children, first of all, being used as profit-making commodities? Second, had the Respondent simply and completely refused to support his children since they moved to London, Ontario, in September 2004? A simple 'YES' to both arms of the second question could justify Child Support Arrears; otherwise, it is nonsensical and could only cement the suspicion in the first question.

These questions easily come up because the Respondent had had to massively support not only the children but also the Applicant without ever thinking in terms of repayment or otherwise. It is the Applicant who single-handedly decided to move to London, Ontario, to take up a professional job there that was more lucrative than the same job she had been offered in Montreal, Quebec. The Applicant decided (there was no discussion of the matter with me) to take the children along to London, Ontario. The Respondent, if he were profit-minded, could have tried to legally stop this move, especially as these children are Quebecois. The Respondent did not stand against this move, entirely cavalier as it was, because he realized that, in the circumstances, it was the best option for the children: more especially in view of the Respondent's uncertain professional and precarious financial situation.

The Respondent was not, and still is not, standing on any firm and comfortable financial grounds from which he could very ably support the children as some of the attached debt reclamations from some official sources can attest to. That is precisely why the Respondent had to take up doing two hard and tedious jobs in the manufacturing industry in 2005 in spite of the very obvious medical and health hazards associated thereto. The second job option has been solely to enable the Respondent to pay off the enormous financial debts, debts incurred largely between 1996 and 2004 during which time both the Applicant and Respondent were studying in Cameroon as well as in Canada.

Without any intervention from any quarter whatsoever, we have a person supporting his one child in the average amount of $300/month with a gross yearly income of $14,839 (2002). In 2003, with a gross annual income of $22,517, this person is willing to support his two children in the average amount of $400/month. Now, is it not simply to grossly ignore the real facts when we say that this same person (while making a gross yearly income of $41,000) has simply refused, pure and pure, to support his two children?

When the Applicant brought this Claim for Divorce, Custody of Children and Child(ren) Support, the Respondent never argued against any of the three. Neither did he contest (as he could have) the use of Ontario Table or Guidelines for determining the amount of child support he should pay, rather than the Guidelines of Quebec where he is resident and which is also the province of origin of the two children. The Respondent again accepted to pay $428/month child support based on a gross yearly income of $28,000 (an amount derived from the average of the three years of 2003-2005). There is just no way (as can be seen from past tax return assessments of 2000-2004) that the Respondent can make $28,000/year from one of the type of jobs he is currently doing. But he has accepted to pay that amount because he knows it is his duty to support his children and, under normal circumstances, no court would even need to tell him to do that.

As I have said earlier, I did not consistently support my children (Ngunyi Ateh-Afac Fossungu and Nguajong

Forbehndia Fossungu) since September 2004 solely because I could not, not that I did not want to. I am ready to continue paying the monthly amount of $428 as agreed until there is a change in my financial and professional position. As the Applicant is insisting on my paying arrears in this regard, I, on my part, here request that this Family Court:

1) Use the Quebec Guidelines instead for determining the amount of child support that I have to pay

2) Order the Applicant to reimburse any child support overpayments made to her in past years (2002-2004)

3) Order the Applicant to repay all the expenses I incurred while she was studying both in Cameroon (University of Buea, 1995-1998) and in Canada (Concordia University & McGill University, 2000-2004). I have some important documents and receipts to support this claim.[50]

You would normally expect any Superior Court of Justice – Family Court, as the one in London which is housed at 80 Dundas Street calls itself, would duly consider these facts and claim of the Respondent when making its decision. Not at all with courts which are just there to do the bidding of scheming women as the London Court that merely mentioned that:

Ms. Asahchop testified that Mr. Fossungu made support payments from time to time. She neglected to bring her records or calculations to trial. Mr. Fossungu failed, as well, to produce any schedules of payment or receipts. He did say "I've been sending cheques when I could." Mr. Fossungu will have to be given credit for the child support he has paid since separation. The parties should sit down and come to an agreement about how much was actually paid. An agreed figure for the

---

[50] Court File # 1162-05, "Child Support Arrears: Give the Respondent a Break".

appropriate credit will have to be given to the Family Responsibility Office in quick order.[51]

The payment schedules together with the copies of cashed cheques were all there in the court file and I just don't understand the judge's claim except in the sense that he never went through the file on which he was making support decision. As a matter of fact, the only credit Justice Vogelsang gave to Mr. Fossungu was just in the saying (from *whatever* the woman admitted). For example, he punished the Respondent for "not produc(ing) his T4 information slips for 2006 or his tax return" on an issue that was not even for the Respondent's proving; but you see him here not doing the same to Ms. Asahchop who "neglected to bring her records or calculations to trial." The judge was instead high-handedly nullifying Madam Justice Blishen[52] without at all even considering (and, perhaps, dismissing) the Respondent's counter-claim for reimbursement that was predicated on the Applicant's demand for arrears; a significant counter-claim that is prominently one of the issues Justice Blishen clearly adjourned to the settlement conference,[53] and not for what Justice Vogelsang was there doing – increasing the child support amount as deceitfully requested by Scholastica.

Whatever the misperception of the child-support-trigger-happy *Vogelsangian* court here, I leave the rest to you and stress only the fact these women (like their *Zigzagging-Vogelsangian* courts) see child support as a means of completely damaging

---

[51] Justice Vogelsang's Endorsement, paragraph 7.

[52] Justice Blishen's judgement of September 26, 2006 ordered "that the Respondent, Peter Ateh-Afac Fossungu, shall pay support to the Applicant, Scholastica Asahchop, for the benefit of the children... in the amount of $428.00 per month, commencing October 1, 2006, being the table amount of child support in accordance with the Child Support Guidelines for an annual income of $28,800.00" (paragraph 3).

[53] "This Court Orders that all other issues particularly the setting of arrears, if any, are adjourned to the Settlement Conference January 15, 2007 at 11.45 A.M" *Id.*, paragraph 4.

the one paying it, not how and whether or not that money is made. You get the matter from one of Scholastica's 'Friendly Reminders' (friendly indeed![54]) to which my response on August 25, 2012 at 12.28 AM was:

Scholastica:

Thank you for the reminder. I just happen to have come to town (not Montreal) today, Friday; otherwise, I might be reading your email long into the future. I am sure if you took the pains back in 2000 to know me and to look

---

[54] On Friday, August 24, 2012 at 12.10 PM Scholastica wrote this "Hello/friendly reminder" to "Hello Dr. Fossungu":

I pray you are doing well with your entire family. You had written an agreement appealing that I should take the child support agreement matter out of the Family and Responsibility office. You indicated at time that you were going to be honouring payments including arrears on your own and did not require the courts in order to do so. I withdrew the matter from court and you honoured the agreement including arrears for the first few months. You later stated that you could not continue with the arrears and I did not complain. You continue to be very inconsistent with the payments and I continue to wonder if you are honouring the agreement? You even notarized the agreement before sending to me. I really struggle with these children on my own and it is not easy. Your daughter was graduating last June and I sent an invitation to you, you mentioned that you will try to come. We neither heard from you nor saw you at the graduation.

I would like you to understand that it is not easy to take care of two children financially, physically and emotionally and I have been trying my best. By the grace of the Almighty God they are doing very well. You daughter is going to middle school and the financial load is quite heavy and I would I like you to keep to the agreement you made when you asked me to withdraw the matter from the Family and Responsibility office. Just to let you know the children are extensively involved in extracurricular activities which does not only leave me with no life of my own, but is very expensive. They are doing very well as a result of all those activities and my relentless efforts. I will like you to see this mail as a genuine appeal /friendly reminder and nothing else. I left you two messages when we came to Montreal but did not hear back from you.

I pray that the good Lord should continue to bless, guide and protect you all, hope to hear from you soon.

Respectfully,

S.A

well ahead as you should have, you would have understood, first, that I am someone who loves honouring my word, the more especially when it has to do with my own children and wife; and, second, that you and I were all that matter to the wellbeing of our children. Yes, I notarized the agreement and that is clear indication of my intention to honour it; but I did not foresee the fluctuations and other imponderables in the type of job I now do and, most importantly, the menace I have lately been getting from some of my creditors.

Scholastica, frankly, do you know what I now do for a living and to pay what I have been paying to you? I am sure if you did you would not be talking of leaving me messages without response. I am in the forest cutting trees, and cut off from the world. Yes, that is what I now do in order not to depend on government last resort assistance. That is the life I now have for having been honest with the woman I love so much and thought love me that much as well.

My dear Scholastica, when I got into the agreement with you, I meant to stick to it all the way. But I am someone who looks at the larger picture and know that sticking to our agreement for a few more months only to end up behind bars is not the best option. If you have a long memory, you will comprehend that I am the last person who would want to bring children into this world and not take care of them. I am almost done with the most threatening of my creditors and will soon get back on track.

Thank you for understanding.

PAF

Yes, these women only see father-and-children in terms of money, never the emotional and other values of that relationship (see Fossungu, 2014: chapters 3 & 4). That is why, while in court, nothing else matters to these gold-diggers and their representatives called Liars (don't be fool also by

'Lawyers'). You can thus see the *zigzagging* one-reason-based decision thesis being also sustained in the fact that, as directed during the previous audience and even by the Monast-judgement they were there in court to set aside,[55] the lawyer never sent his client's revenue documentation to Peter like truthful Peter did send his to the Liar (examples are in various email communications in an earlier chapter). That is why the lawyer already had all his calculated child support amounts stored up in his mobile phone and was just pouring them out to the judge who, on his part, saw nothing wrong when Peter raised the issue. Would you categorize it as Ignorance of the Facts or Judicial Bias? You also see the lawyer solely deciding the case in the double payments I have to make to both the *sole custodian* and *the day-care*. Never seen wonders? Then quickly migrate to Quebec! So, I should obviously be paying the day-care for one of the London children too, right? *Zigzaggism* is purely Quebec based, I guess? A silly question, I further guess, if you wonder what the real difference is between *Zigzaggism* and *Vogelsangism*. Why then have family law as a federal matter if such variations do exist in Canada? But not when it comes to enforcing child support? So many endless queries but let's remain with this one: What then was the rationale for rebranding SCPCS to *sole custody* if Peter still had to do all those things he was already doing under SCPCS? Money-Only sole custody! Gold-digging at its *gravelling* zenith!

All the irregularities I am affixing to the *Zigzagging* Judgement would be heavily sustained by even a very casual look at the *procès-verbal* of the two verdicts. Remember that the stenographer sets down what goes on, not what the *gravelling* and *zigzagging* team would instruct him/her to put down. Table 1 gives you an idea of the laughing-stock nature of the hearing of March 6 juxtaposed with the one it cancelled.

---

[55] "**ORDONNE** aux parties de se communiquer mutuellement leur déclaration de revenu dans un délai de 15 jours."

Table 1: Comparison of Stenographers' Notes of Procès-Verbal d'Audience

Relevant Item(s)	Justice Michèle MONAST & the SCPCS Decision of April 24, 2014	Justice Jerry ZIGMAN & the Sole Custody Decision of March 6, 2015
Début	14h28	9h19
Fin	14h55	10h56
	Ouverture de l'audience	Ouverture de l'audience (9h19)
	Identification de la cause et des parties	Identification de la cause et des parties (9h20)
	Représntation de Me Gravel	Echange entre le tribunal et le procureur et le défendeur (9h20)
	Echanges de part et d'autre	
Suspension	14h35	9h41
Reprise	15h47	10h02
	Echange avec le TRIBUNAL	Preuve en demande (10h04)
Start time of Decision	15h52	10h52
10h04		Témoin 1 – Bayiha
10h05		Interrogation de Me Gravel
10h11		Me Gravel produit la déclaration de revenu de madame
10h13		Interrogation du défendeur
		Preuve en demande close
10h16		Preuve en défense –

		Fossungu
10h17		Le défendeur s'adresse au Tribunal
10h51		Preuve close de la part et d'autre
10h52		Jugement

If I may reiterate, add to that the fact that Judge Zigman in his decision-making relied solely on "the *reason* given in presence of the parties and recorded" (my emphasis), never anything whatsoever that was in the court file before him. Thus, the decision of Judge Monast had no bearing on the March 6 farcical ruling. You just cannot be a judge overruling a previous ruling without clearly stating the reasons for doing so; and you cannot be able to do that until you discuss that previous ruling. Well, I wouldn't want to say anymore here since you already have all the facts before you and can decide what you think of them. The one thing I need to precise is this. Perhaps the judge and lawyer were doing all that because they did not see me as a lawyer or someone who could even know what was going on? Judging the book by its colour! As I have said, it is even the woman's lawyer who calculated the support amount all the time and the judges simply imposed it *in toto*. It was a real drama on March 6, with me (who was representing myself) just being a mere spectator almost entirely since the judge constantly shut me up (with "Don't argue with me or you'll be sorry!") whenever I tried to insist on raising an objection to the farce.

Here then are some issues drawn from Fossungu (2015b: 191-193) for your further review. Is it normal for the court to be according sole custody to a parent who is on welfare and with a precarious situation in Canada *against* the request of the other parent who is self-supporting and willing to raise the kids without depending on welfare? Is it right for me to be paying children support to a *full custodian* of our two children *and* still

98

be additionally responsible for paying the day-care expenses of one of these children? Does the Montreal Family High Court actually understand what a decree of full custody means? Would I be violating the law or not: if (for instance) I stand in the way of my ex-partner's move to change the children's day-care provider? And what about my refusing to pay any amount more or less than $158.16 to whatever the day-care is? There are a lot of puzzles in this judgement that was evidently rendered without considering all the facts presented by me and without putting the best interest of the children on the table. You and I can see some of these theses being validated in the effects of parents' and institutions' gross errors on blameless children.

Effects Of Parents'/Institutions' Errors On Innocent Children

Here I will make the point with two main issues: (1) the day-care saga and *gravellism* and (2) *Odettooldism* and the *Kelielization* of the CIC Heartlessness.

The Day-Care Saga and *Gravelism* Mating with the *Scholapeterist* Lecture on Children's Best Interest?

As soon as she left the court smiling so broadly with her new children-screwing powers, Flavie went quickly to the day-care to inform Filomena how she is now the sole custodian of the children. Filomena had immediately reminded her how that means she (Flavie) would be the one now to sign the children's day-care papers and Flavie had then cried out to her that the papers should be sent to Peter who has been signing them. Yeah! Money-only sole custody! When I had raised this particular issue in court, her lawyer quickly indicated that she has had her situation regularized. No documentation tendered to or required by the judge. And about her asking for sole custody without having a job, the lawyer pointed out she was receiving welfare (that is certainly the regularization the lawyer means? No evidence of this also required?). Yet, the courts of Canada would side-step a parent who is not dependent on the state for everything and not also demanding child support from *their* own dependant and go on to tie two innocent children to an incapable parasite. Someone that the state itself, for that matter, does not recognize as capable or entitled to do this and that for the children! The Canadian system couldn't get a lot more interesting for my itchy pen! Just listen to lawyers who are supposed to put the lay person through some of these legal niceties.

On April 1, 2015, I received this *mise en demeure* dated 13 March 2015 from Me. Gravel (the same lawyer who announced Flavie's regularized situation in court on 6 March), sent by registered mail. The Gravel mail read:

> Monsieur, Notre cliente, Madame Henriette Flavi Bayiha, nous informe de ce que suit. Vous refusez et ou négligez de signer les formulaires pour qu'elle puisse inscrire les enfants à la garderie sur la rue de la Savanne à Montréal.
>
> Depuis le jugement du 6 mars 2015, dont vous trouverez copie, vous avez l'obligation légale de payer les frais de garderie de l'enfant Peter et par le fait même de faire tout en votre pouvoir pour que les enfants puissent continuer de fréquenter ladite garderie.
>
> En conséquence, nous vous mettons en demeure de signer tous les documents nécessaires à la garderie que vos enfants fréquentent dans les dix jours de la présente. À défaut par vous d'obtempérer, nous serons dans l'obligation de prendre les procédures judiciaires qui s'imposent dans un tel cas sans autres avis, ni délai.
>
> VEUILLEZ AGIR EN CONSÉQUENCE
> BILODEAU ET GRAVEL
> Par: Patrice Gravel, avocat-médiateur

(You will fully grasp this French passage through reading up to my response to it below.) Yeah Lecturer Scholastica of London! Did you by any means forget to inform your Montreal students that I have nothing whatsoever to do with the registration and contract-signing of the children's day-care/schooling in London? Lawyer Gravel is calling it "formulaire" with a purpose. It is contract (*le contrat*). Didn't I already talk about the 'Quebec Gang of Liars' to you? I only received the above note (together with another registered mail from the day-care provider, Filomena Pina Gonzalez, probably being the day-care contract papers) on April 1, 2015. As you have heard already, Filomena's was never opened and was returned (hand delivered) the same day to Filomena by me who was very disappointed in Filomena's attitude because she knows as well as any Quebec day-care provider that at this point I have no authority to sign the papers just as I have none before Revenue Canada/Quebec as far as any children money from them is concerned. Remember the reason for the consensual agreement that even led to this court suit? It was all Revenue Canada-related, provoked by Flavie insisting on and actually declaring her taxes separately while we were still living together and with children (see Fossungu, 2015a: 60-61). Here is my *lapidationistic* response on April 1, 2015 to *Gravelism*:

Sir: I have just received today your letter of 13 March 2015. Let me inform you that the court decision you enclosed in it was also seen.

The Montreal Family High Court has my contact information and, henceforth, it is from it that I should be receiving any instructions relating to the decision it rendered on March 6, 2015. It is clearly not your place to be giving me any instructions and lectures. You are neither the court nor my lawyer. I represented myself in court and can equally read and understand the court's decision.

I am just wondering if, as the lawyer that you are, you do at all comprehend the meaning of the SOLE CUSTODY that you and your client went to and got from the court. If you think that you can intimidate me to violate a court order, you had better think again.

I will be on the watch for "les procédures judiciaries" you are talking about, and let that come directly from the court. Just don't send any more menaces to me.

Thank you.

Sincerely yours,

Peter Ateh-Afac FOSSUNGU

As I mentioned earlier, this Montreal Family Court behaved all along as if Patrice Gravel was a two-party lawyer; ignoring me and taking only what the lawyer said. For instance, as I took the oath and was providing my address, I was asked to cut it short. Asking later how my communications could reach me without the postal code, for example, the response was that "Me. Gravel would send the procès-verbal to you by email". I never had the court decision until April 1, 2015; all this notwithstanding my March 2015 letter to that court in which I clearly made it known that I was adult enough to receive correspondence from the court directly through my various contact methods (postal address, email, phone) fully specified therein. One would be entitled to wonder if, in stating in court that Ms. Bayiha had regularized her situation, her lawyer had the best interests of the children at all anywhere in his head. And this is one reason why I usually don't like involving these professionals in my family matters.

For illustration, I will first take you back to London's *Asahchop v. Fossungu* to also cement the thesis that knowing yourself and situation makes solving problems confronting you easier (see Fossungu, 2013: chapter 1). Validating it in regard of *Asahchop v. Fossungu*, because I knew myself and what I was up against, I also could afford to disagree with the numerous demands of all the professionals when Scholastica '*cunny-manly*' sued. People of the law and other social scientists kept pushing and saying I should get a lawyer to represent me. I did not do so because I (very unlike any lawyer I could have hired) knew exactly what the real issue was. It was only the personal interest of Scholastica and those of her brothers, sisters, and parents that would belie the court case, not those of the children; and the said interests she has been out to secure using the children and courts were long decided upon before she ever landed in Canada. I do have some of the letters from her parents and siblings to her that do also attest to this thesis.[56] *En plus*, even if a London lawyer was acquainted with the facts, he or she would still have dramatized them the lawyerly way to make more money, without bothering so much about the children's future and interests as I do – the *Bayiha* lawyer's comportment attesting a 100%. That necessarily takes us momentarily back to Montreal.

---

[56] For a small illustration, in Scholastica's father's letter of October 9, 2002 to Scholastica they were discussing her numerous plans of sending her junior brother, Eugene Lekeawung Asahchop, to further his medical school studies in Belgium as well as of bringing several of her family members (siblings and parents) to Canada. I don't usually go nosing for information about people; but I knew all this because the secret letters usually miraculously came to my attention. Thus, while in Cameroon, in late October 2002 Eugene was following me all around the place (to Yaoundé especially) preparing his Belgium documents without telling me about it, but not knowing that I was actively aiding him in the matter, knowing all the same. He must have been taking me for the real fool that their entire family would take me for. But the conscience of people like this would never allow them to do things normally, explaining the young man's comportment when he eventually crossed over to Montreal. And there is also this other guy called Dr. Magnus Ajong who usually did most of the money transfers (Canada-Belgium) during his numerous trips to Canada and to our LaSalle residence. He still thinks to date that I was clearly unaware of the behind-my-back dealings. I used to just look at all of them and just laugh inside because, as I have theorized (see Fossungu, 2014: 75), the best way to understand just how far others would go on taking you for a fool is to assume the position of an idiot.

In the evening of Friday, May 8, 2015 Filomena P. Gonzalez called me to talk about her frustration with the way the children are being brought to and taken from her by Flavie. They often (if not always) come in without having taken breakfast; dirty and unkempt; late; and without necessary clothing that she has long been requesting for. How they often arrive crying because (as they later often explain to her) their mother regularly hits them, even in the bus, etc. How, on leaving the day-care, they are usually asked by their mother to run (unaccompanied) in order to catch the bus; and how Peteraf almost got run down by a vehicle in the process. That their mother would not heed to advice from her not to let the children run on the streets like that. That it has gotten to an unsettling point where she had no choice but to involve child protection officials because she is enormously concerned about the children's safety and wellbeing. I was listening to her lengthy narration of the dangers to the children that evening in tears because I knew it was exactly the fate the *zigzagging-gravelling* Court had spelled for them on March 6, 2015.

And, frankly, on Tuesday, May 19, 2015 I also got a confirming call from a Montreal Youth Protection official called Stepanie Paquette who was trying to understand the situation of my children. As she explained to me, she is now the one charged with my children's case. She posed a lot of questions and I told her I could only talk about what I know for sure. That is, from 2009 until the March 6, 2015 court decision that surprisingly ignored all what I had warned the court about (and which the Youth Protection official was also very concerned about), in regard of the children. Stepanie Paquette was just as surprised to learn that the court was acquainted with all these facts but still went ahead to grant sole custody to Flavie. She promised to do everything in her powers to ensure that the children are well taken care of; also requesting that I should call her any time if I have any concerns, etc. But what fears can I now have that would be any different from those the court ignominiously ignored in March 2015? In other words, the persistent question remains that of whether the Quebec Montreal Court really had to put these innocent children through all the hell they are now going through.[57] And, is the Montreal Incapable Student emulating the Accomplished London Teacher well, with the help of uninformed lawyers?

Do remember the arguments of the head of the sciences department of Cameroon College of Arts and Sciences (CCAS) Kumba why I should stay in sciences (Fossungu, 2013: 60). Very coherent as it was, it did not factor in my unique situation which I alone understood and I therefore refused to give in to his persuasion. Had I therefore tried to lawyer-fight Scholastica on the custody and child support grounds in the London court, the children could surely have ended up in a public institution or other foster home. I love my children so much that I would rather see them growing up with their mother (scheming as she may be) than in a foster home or other public institution. That

---

[57] On Friday 29 May 2015 I called the day-care to find out what the payment for next month (June) will be so that I could drop the cheque in the mail. Filomena instead was narrating to me that, since Tuesday May 26, 2015 they have ceased attending her day-care because their mother has been lying to her a lot and, as things currently stand, she (Filomena) cannot get her money (about $3000.00) paid to her because Flavie has so far not been able to furnish even her refugee papers that the paying authority has accepted to examine and decide if it can entitle Flavie to sign the day-care contract! Many other incomprehensible acts of Flavie's, including her serving the day-care provider with a letter that attempts to prohibit Filomena from allowing me to come to the daycare to see the children, or talk to them on the phone while they are there: without Flavie's express authorization. Well, others may be astonished here. Not me. I saw it coming long, long time ago, even during the JCA's operation. Else, how do we explain Flavie's jealously guarding the children's documents to the extent that she would rather see them dead than let me have their medical cards for the purpose of taking them to the clinic – whereas she herself would not do so but keep lying about having taken them to hospital?

105

is why, absent the Criminal Love Theory, these Child-Support Business School graduates (passing for loving mothers) would have known that Peter Ateh-Afac Fossungu just does not even need the court to order for any child support for him to support his children; nor would he do that simply to impress others. All this and more is pellucid enough from my instructive 'Hi Scholastica' Letter of October 13, 2003 that sensible students of Children's Best Interests plainly can't afford to do without:

I hear you always boasting around the whole place that you are the incarnation of the best interest of our children. Go on saying whatever you will but here is what I (and, of course, reasonable and right-thinking people with the hard facts) would make of it. The best interest and wellbeing of these children are not at all concepts that figure anywhere in your thinking and demeanour. It is only the furthering of your selfish interests <u>through</u> these children that you are always wrapping up as your belaboured concern for their wellbeing. Otherwise, we wouldn't now be living apart in the first place and, second, you wouldn't be threatening me with the courts that, according to you, are going to "make things clear" to us regarding our children whose wellbeing is your other name. (I have got your voicemail to this effect on tape) As you do think that the arrangement, including the financial, that we already have is not clear, be advised then that I am putting a STOP-PAYMENT on some of the cheques I gave you in July 2003 – that is, those for the months of November 2003 (cheque N° 754 of $400) and of December 2003 (cheque N° 755 of $600) – until you have brought the court action for the clarification as per your threat. I sent you my complete postal address on receipt of your threat and I am still waiting to be duly served with documentation regarding the said legal proceedings.

One very basic thing that you fail to grasp is that only offenders would tremble at the mention of the courts, not law-abiding people. Again you woefully lack understanding that if I do not merit a little bit of respect and encouragement from you for any other reason (and there are very many reasons) I do deserve them for the mere fact that I am the father of the two children that you do unnecessarily claim to be doing everything for, all by yourself. I am very sure you will now actually be able to authentically do all for them by yourself because, until I hear from the courts, I do not know exactly what my role in these children's life is: especially as in your threatening voicemail you clearly prohibited me from coming to your residence to see them "just whenever you like". Furthermore, on the morning of Saturday 11 October 2003 (yesterday) I called you to arrange how and when to pick the children and all that I got from you was that I was doing so in order to "cover up" since it was our "meeting day". I don't truly know what "cover up" you are referring to. I have never believed that outsiders can always know better than parents what is in the best interest of their child. But faced with the kind of situation you are presenting, I think I must agree with you now that a court with the straight facts can do better. Should the court decide that you will do better than me having the kids, then it will also decide what my role generally or specifically towards the children will be, or vice versa. You cannot be separated and get the advantages of separation and at the same time be craving for the advantages of living together. That is just not possible my dear know-all wife. You just can't go on forever making the entire world revolve around your desires, Period.

Signed

Dr. Nkemtale'eh P.A. Fossungu

There is no better *periodization* for this essential lecture than my other 'Hi' Letter of November 12, 2005 to Scholastica (which you would better also read as a general response to all her so-called 'friendly reminders' on child-support since the time of her court-given rights – and plenty of evidence to also prop up the Scheming Theory[58]). I indicated in that note in all-capitals that:

I DON'T NEED YOU TO TELL ME HOW, WHEN, & WHERE, TO LOOK AFTER MY CHILDREN. ON THE OTHER HAND, I DON'T DO WHAT I CANNOT DO JUST TO PLEASE OTHER PEOPLE. I DO WHAT I CAN DO, WHEN I CAN DO IT, AND WHERE I CAN DO THAT. SO, JUST STOP PESTERING ME: FOR DOING SO IS NEVER GOING TO MAKE ME DO WHAT I CANNOT DO, WHEN I CANNOT DO IT, NO MATTER WHAT.

I KNOW EXACTLY WHAT I HAVE TO DO. AND I DO IT WHEN I CAN DO IT.

FOR YOUR INFORMATION: KNOW THAT NO COURT CAN MAKE ME, IN VIEW OF WHAT I MAKE AS INCOME NOW, TO MAKE A PAYMENT OF TWO HUNDRED DOLLARS A MONTH FOR TWO CHILDREN. BUT I DON'T NEED ANY COURT TO ORDER ME TO MAKE THAT AMOUNT AVAILABLE TO MY CHILDREN – KNOWING FULLY THAT THIS CAN NEVER EVER MAKE UP FOR WHAT THEY ARE ENORMOUSLY MISSING.

ENCLOSED, YOU WILL FIND TWO CHEQUES.

---

[58] "But why do some of these people just never get it? That is, to live with someone for so long and yet cannot get the smallest clue as to who he/she is? It may surprise others; not me, because I understand this one thing. When you are in a relationship with a hidden agenda, you cannot see what you should have seen, since you see only your scheming as *everything*" (Fossungu, 2015a: 69, emphasis is original).

Signed

Coming back squarely on the issue of financial support, as the Respondent had argued in the London court, "I think it is one thing to say that someone's financial support is not enough but quite another thing to suggest that s/he is not supporting at all. Unfortunately, I used to rely on the Applicant's good faith and did not keep copies of the cheques initially and sometimes even gave cash instead. While wondering where the Applicant would be today had this same 'It's-Only-Me-That-Must-Matter' attitude of hers been adopted by the mother of the other child in Douala, Cameroon, I will simply say nothing more on this issue other than to refer you to the attached copies of some of the cheques (including two notes from me to her in their regard) that were given to the Applicant during the period of separation."[59] Talking about the mother of the other child in Douala brings us to squarely focus on *Odettitooldism* and the CIC heartlessness.

Odettitooldism and the *Kelielization* of the CIC Heartlessness: What Has the Child Done Wrong to Carry the Cross Forever?

"You will discover the proper meaning of *odettitooldism* by finding and meeting that unique woman in this world that refuses a man proposing marriage to her solely because 'I'm too old for you'"(Fossungu, 2014: 135). I have a daughter (Kelie) who has been blocked in Cameroon until this moment that we speak by the heartlessness of Citizenship and Immigration Canada (CIC) because of the error of parents (Odette (& Peter?)) that is hinged on the claim of loving and protecting a child more than the other parent can do. Listen to

---

[59] *Asahchop v. Fossungu*, "Putting the Facts Straight," p.3. All that is there in the file and yet Judge Vogelsang says otherwise.

the story of an innocent child who, according to CIC, just has to suffer for the rest of her life for the 'sins' of her parents: despite the determined efforts of a parent to put things right. In late 2010, I sponsored Kelie under the Family Class with CIC confirming receipt of the Application on January 10, 2011. On September 28, 2011 CIC rejected the Application on the basis that I was not found eligible to sponsor her as a daughter because she never featured in my own application for permanent residence made in 2001.[60] Despite (1) all the explanations I made regarding her not featuring in my own application and (2) our willingness to establish our daughter-father relationship by DNA Testing, CIC's *Roundaboutism* has heartlessly stood in the way.

Odettitooldism: What Explanation Is Enough Explanation?

After receiving CIC's first letter of September 28, 2011, in my letter of October 8, 2011 with subject title "RE: KELIE TSOPZEM FOSSUNGU" I attempted acquainting the Department with the hard reality of the case as follows. I would prefer to give you the letter verbatim although a large part of it is already published in my other books.

Dear Sir/Madam,

---

[60] "This refers to the Application to Sponsor a Member of the Family Class you submitted to this office on behalf of KELIE FOSSUNGU TSOPZEM and family (if applicable). We have reviewed your application and regret to advise that you are not an eligible sponsor for the following reason(s): You have not submitted an application for a member of the family class. You did not declare the applicant to Citizenship and Immigration Canada on your own Application for Permanent Residence or at the time you became permanent resident of Canada. As such, you do not meet regulation 117(9Xd). Please refer to the Immigration and Refugee Protection Regulations listed below for details." CIC Letter of September 28, 2011 to me.

110

I have received your correspondence of 28 September 2011 in which you notified me of the decision concerning Kelie Tsopzem Fossungu whom I applied to sponsor as my child under the *catégorie du regroupement familial.* You are quite right that she has never figured in my file as my child. I think, from hindsight, that my main error has been that of not having included an explanatory note as the present with the application, especially in support of my request for the DNA. It was not a deliberate error, and neither was my never mentioning her during the two occasions you alluded to, a lie on my part – all being tied to what I would describe below as a gross error on her mother's part. It is my belief however that this child (like any other) is not to be the one to pay for the (largely inadvert) errors of the parent(s): the driving force behind this note.

By the time I came to Canada in September 1995 I had no knowledge that I had any child. It was the same in September 1991 (my very first arrival here). That is precisely why your records do not bear any indication of my having any child then.

It was in the year 2000 that knowledge of this child (Kelie) came to me [Actually it is 1998: with 2000 being the year I first discussed the issue with anyone ever]. I was then very confused and shocked by (rather than being glad at) the news. Why was I only learning of the existence of my daughter then? Kelie's mother happens to be the aunt of my wife (Scholastica Asahchop) who had just arrived Canada the year before (1999). That is why, she had explained, she had kept the child's paternity a secret, even to me till then. (You can see that Kelie's *initial* birth certificate that was eventually presented to me – copy enclosed – bears but the name of her mother's late husband who had died before 1993 when I first met her.) She had pleaded with me to keep [Kelie's] true paternity

111

just between her and myself. But I did not see why that should be so and told her so.

On recovering from the shock and confusion and after serious consideration of the obvious complications, I sat my wife down one day and broke the news to her, trying to reason with her as follows: You and I can actually choose who to have as a spouse; but a child never has that choice of who the parents are to be. Therefore, if Kelly is my daughter as I think she is (since viewing the whole messy situation we were in I do not think her mother would be joking about it), then I have to necessarily assume my responsibilities towards her as a father. This is what I must have to do, with you (my wife) only having the choice of deciding whether I do so *within* or *without* our marriage.

My wife said she was to think about it but her attitude thereafter indicated to me that, by being frank in discussing the matter with her, I had spelt the end of the marriage. But she apparently had made up her mind not to go right away but only after five years when she must have first put me into a deep hole. For instance, she had two children with me solely to use (after I must have gone down deep into debts footing the bills and taking care of a four-member family all alone until she had finished her schooling as a social worker) in her divorce and child custody and support suit in 2005. All this happened solely because I was truthful about Kelie (Kelly, as I knew it then), a fact that is largely responsible, directly and indirectly, for a holder of a doctorate degree in law now working in the forest. It would have been different if my wife had been serious about sponsoring me to become a permanent resident, as I would have been one not very long after graduating in December 2000. You know Canadian immigration regulations well enough to understand the rest of the story: Jobs in my field (university lecturer) are directed only to Canadian citizens and

112

permanent residents; and to become a permanent resident, I would need to show that I have that job. Well, I had to pass through my own request for asylum that was initiated in March 2000, leading to permanent residence, a process that took quite some time.

But the important issue here is: **Why was Kelie not included in my application then?** It was because the only information I had about her (until a few months to the initiation of this application for her sponsorship) was that she was called Kelly. This is where what I have referred to above as the 'gross error' of her mother comes in. Despite all my effort, from when I learnt of her being my daughter, to obtain her basic information (e.g., full name, date of birth and/or copy of birth certificate), her mother never let me have it: always claiming that her child would be endangered – 'killed', as she put it – if she came to Canada. I tried several times, in vain, to talk her out of this silly idea; and emphasizing that Canada was not like Cameroon. Time was fast running out on me (with one-entry student visa) and I had no other option then but to file my applications (asylum & residence) without Kelly. Now, would CIC not have considered me insane or abnormal if in those applications I had merely indicated having a daughter in Cameroon whose only details I had was "Kelly"? If I did not hide Kelie's existence to my wife in order to keep my marriage (and professional advancement) intact, there is absolutely no reason on earth that I would then be withholding it from CIC (Citizenship and Immigration Canada) but for the absence of the necessary information to back it up. This is the more especially so as I was entering Canada as a Principal, and not being sponsored by someone else (like my wife who already knew about it anyways); and as it would have been so easy (if I then had the necessary information on hand) to have entered together with Kelie then.

As a permanent resident and citizen, I have even made three trips to Cameroon (2002, 2004, & 2007) during which I always thought I could, in person, talk some sense into Kelie's mother and obtain the required information and documentation. The three times I was still unsuccessful. I have even also tried passing through Kelie's senior half-brother, Eclador Tsafack, through emails (some copies enclosed) to obtain her information as well as that of her other siblings. What else have I not done in this regard? It was not until sometime late in 2010 that (while on the phone with her, Henriette Flavie Bayiha – my common law partner – asked me if she could personally talk to her and I handed her the phone and) Flavie lengthily talked to Kelie's mother, woman-to-woman, that she began opening up and cooperating in the matter.

When I finally got hold of the initial birth certificate enclosed, all I requested her to do (if she knew, as only her could until the DNA testing, I was indeed the father) was to go back to the issuing office and explain things out so that they could issue a new one that carried my information as the biological father. I made this demand principally so that the child's travelling documents (passport) could be established using the corrected certificate (also enclosed here, as was in the application).

Please, I myself doubt parts of this child's information that has been passed on to me, especially the year of birth. Could her mother have perhaps used 1997 simply to eliminate any possible suspicions of those close to her that I (then the husband of her niece) was her daughter's father: since I had left Cameroon in September 1995? I do not comprehend a lot regarding the alterations that might have taken place in her efforts to keep the child's true paternity a secret. But the important thing to me is that Kelie is the innocent and deserving person in the mess that I have been plunged into and, trust me, I made a firm commitment in

2000 to be there for this girl, my first child ever, as the DNA testing that I requested in the application would have to confirm. In short, I am simply tired of 'running' three homes (Montreal, London, & Douala) in two different countries and just want now to have the opportunity of bringing up *all* my children together and in this wonderful country that I have since chosen to spend the rest of my life in. Your counsel as to how I should proceed with Kelie's case is highly solicited.

Thanks a lot for your comprehension and direction.

Yours sincerely,
Peter Ateh-Afac Fossungu [bold is original]

Updating Family and the Second Sponsorship

On February 7, 2012 I sent CIC a letter in which I notified it of 'additions to my family' that listed the three children born "after I became a permanent resident in March 2002" as well as Kelie who obviously "was already born by the time I was applying for permanent residence but at that time I did not have her information to have included her then in my file. **I am hereby requesting therefore that she also be added to my file: pending DNA confirmation**. Thank you for your comprehension." (Bold is original) The CIC's response to this Notification came in on March 5, 2012 with Kelie's returned birth certificate, advising that

This letter refers to your correspondence dated February 07, 2012 in which you write that you wish to add Kelie Fossungu Tsopzem to your application for permanent residence.

Please note that once a decision is rendered on an application for Permanent Residence, it cannot be re-opened to add dependents.

115

If you wish to sponsor Kelie, you are required to submit a completed sponsorship application kit including the processing fees in effect at the time of the submission......

A very good piece of *doublesidism* in a sense, that is. Encouragement and disappointment all bundled up, you are pondering? For me, there was only encouragement because no disappointment was ever going to break my commitment to my children. That is why I made another Sponsorship Application which included this letter dated April 26, 2012 with its subject line being "WILLINGNESS TO UNDERGO DNA BLOOD TESTING". Dear Sir/Madam, it announced,

I wish to inform you that Kelie Fossungu Tsopzem and I are willing to undergo DNA Blood Testing as part of the sponsorship application I am here making in her favour under the Family Class. We are ready to follow this course since we do not have the necessary documentation to easily establish our relationship of father and daughter and also to speed up our application.

Sincerely yours,

Peter Ateh-Afac Fossungu

This second Application was in April 2012 and one would normally have received an acknowledgement of its receipt about a month at the most. Not so with this case. I began wondering what the problem might be and thought it could be related to the DNA question. Could it be because I never included the test with the application? Don't think so, as CIC would have indicated that to me, at least. Whatever the case, I told myself, I need to do something. On Sunday, September 29, 2012 6:22 AM, I wrote to a DNA testing establishment called WARNEX services PRO-ADN (Julie Beauchamp representing in customer service), stating "Hi: I need DNA testing for immigration purpose (sponsorship of daughter who is in Douala, Cameroon). I am in Montreal, Quebec. Please, I need an appointment and other information as to how to go about it. Thanks. Peter." I got Julie's response on Monday, October 1, 2012 at 1.40 PM. Thanking me for choosing **WARNEX PRO-DNA Services.**, she advised that for customers wishing to undergo the DNA test for immigration purposes, "you must provide us with a letter from CIC (Citizenship and Immigration Canada) stating which relationship must be established. We will refer you to one of our collection centres near you in Canada where you will be asked to present official identification with a photograph (ex. driver's licence, medical card, etc.) and supply us with two (2) recent photographs (passport-size and quality), after which the samples will follow a strict chain of custody. We will also contact the Embassy for the other participant(s) of the test and provide them with all the necessary material for the DNA sample collection as well as instructions and consent forms."

I then narrated to Julie on Monday, October 8, 2012 at 3.52 PM that "I have been looking for the letter from CIC since we last talked and found it only today. It is here attached. My phone number is 438-381-1676 or 514-418-3639. Looking forward to hearing from you. Peter." The letter I attached to Julie's email communication was CIC's letter of September 28, 2011 (the negative response). The next day at 4.09 PM Julie made it clear that the CIC letter I had sent to them was not the right one since "We are looking for a letter from High Commission of Canada in the country where is the child requesting a DNA test." It was certainly becoming more complicated than I had envisioned. I then sent word to Kelie's brother in Douala (on Sunday, October 13, 2012 at 9.15 AM), asking him to "Please see if you can arrange to have an appointment with the Canadian Embassy in Yaoundé for the purpose of having a DNA testing for Kelie. If you can call them first to have information on what to do then let me know so that we can have this issue resolved. It is all the fault of your mother who does not want to see things in light of the benefit of her own children. Just imagine where all of you would be today if Kelie was here since 2000 and you would know what I am talking about. Anyway, let's see what we can do; better late than never. PAF" On Monday, October 13, 2012 at 10.11 AM I sent the CIC letter to Valery Stey of Maxxam as per the phone discussion I had with her. Having read from Valery, I had to inform Kelie's brother not to bother contacting the embassy because they were to be the ones to contact him or the mother (through their phone numbers) in case the embassy need them to proceed. That was on Monday, October 15, 2012 at 11.12 AM.

With all the unusual silence from CIC and the crazy back and forth DNA confusion still puzzling and going on, on October 14, 2012, using the address of her secondary school (discovered from the application forms filled over there in Douala), I sent a letter by post to 'My dear daughter, Kelie', stating that:

> I write this letter to you (the very first) with a lot of tears. Tears because I know both you and I are not supposed to be in the situation in which we are right now. Until now I have tried to do things through your mother but they have not been working as should be because she does not seem to be looking at your future and that of your other siblings. To your mother you may be the last child but you are my first child, with four others behind you (a half-sister and three half-brothers). I am writing this letter because I think at your age I can now deal with you directly to make sure that you can come to Canada and take advantage of the endless opportunities here. If you can communicate with me through email that will be fine but here is my complete contact information:

118

Email: pafossungu@yahoo.ca Phone: 438-381-1676; 514-418-3639. Postal Address: Dr. Peter A. Fossungu, 325-7225 Rue De Nancy, Montreal, Quebec, H3R 2L8 CANADA [paragraphing altered here]

I love you, my daughter, and I am looking forward to reading or hearing from you.

Dr. Peter A. Fossungu

P/S: Do take your English lessons very seriously because you will be needing them here. Although Canada is bilingual (English and French), English is largely spoken in North America.

The Golden Plus Three Gift: The *CICization* of Slumber or *Tremblaybullshitation*?

It looks like CIC had gone to sleep and needed to be made to wake up. Was it natural or usual doze off or deliberate inaction akin to the *tremblaybullshiting*? Whatever it was, I am not sure.[61] But, having waited until then without hearing a

---

[61] My mother's own Sponsorship Application was made in 2010. But until I informed CIC in late 2014 that she died in June 2014, the first and last communication I ever received on the issue is this letter of January 10, 2011 that acknowledged receipt without ever even mentioning her name:

This letter is to confirm receipt of the Application to Sponsor a Member of the Family Class that you have submitted. Please note that any co-signer and/or dependents listed on your application will only be added to your file once processing has begun.

Please be advised that except for sponsorships for spouses and dependent children, there is a longer processing time for all other members of the family class e.g. parents and grandparents, than has been experienced in the past.

Canada has long been a country of choice for many immigrants. This is due, in part, because we have a successful and carefully balanced program that is based on three concepts: immigrants who can contribute to our economy, reunification of families, and refugees and those in need of protection.

Having a successful immigration program means that we aim to maintain a balance of economic to non-economic applicants that will most benefit Canada. As such, we are committed to keeping the proportion of

thing from CIC on the Kelie file, on October 23, 2012, I therefore sent them the following letter that had as subject "A

---

economic immigrants as close as possible to our targeted 60%, and our non-economic immigrants to 40%.

The Economic Class is made up of people such as skilled workers and business immigrants, and the Non-Economic Category is made up of Family Class immigrants and those in need of protection.

In the Family Class, the Government of Canada is committed to reuniting close family members first, which means that we process spouses, partners and dependent children on a priority basis. Currently, CIC processes 50% of these applications in six months or less, and 80% in under 12 months.

Given the importance of meeting our target of economic immigrants, the goals of our humanitarian program, and the priority we place on processing close family members first, we have to make difficult choices. This means that, at this time, applicants in the parents and grandparents category are experiencing longer processing times.

All sponsorship applications for parents and grandparents are being processed by the Case Processing Centre in Missisauga according to the date the complete application was received in this office. The processing time for sponsorship applications are available at the following link: http://www.cic.gc.ca/english/information/times/canada/process-in.asp. This site is updated regularly so you will always have access to current processing times.

We understand that longer processing times can be frustrating for those seeking to bring family members to Canada, but we hope that this information will help explain the delays that you are experiencing when sponsoring parents and grandparents. We understand the wishes of sponsors to have their parents join them and we strive to balance this with a number of competing priorities.

Please be aware that you have the option to withdraw your application at any point in the process, and you **may** be eligible for a refund of the sponsorship fee and/or the permanent resident application fees if processing has not begun on your file.

If you require information about Immigration programs and services please visit our website at www.cic.gc.ca or contact the Citizenship and Immigration Call Centre toll-free at 1-888-242-2100.

In closing, please ensure that you report any changes to your address immediately to the Call Centre or notify this office via mail at the above noted address or by fax at 905-803-7392. Incorrect or old addresses may result in delays in the processing of your application.

Officer DP
Case Processing Centre
Missisauga

120

REQUEST FOR DNA TESTING REQUEST LETTER".
Addressed to Dear Sir/Madam, it read:

Subsequent to your decision of 28 September 2011, I sent in a sponsorship application again in favour of my daughter, KelieTsopzem Fossungu, indicating that I would like to use DNA in proof of my being her father. Until this moment I have not heard anything from your office nor received a letter requesting for the DNA test. I have been trying to have that test but cannot because I am told it cannot be done without a letter from your office requesting for it. I am therefore requesting that you send me the said letter.

Thank you. Sincerely, Peter A. Fossungu [paragraphing altered for this line].

This particular letter was returned to me by CIC with stamp on it showing that it was received on October 25, 2012 at Case Processing Centre Missisauga (CPC-M). The CIC undated 2-page letter accompanying it merely said in the first paragraph that "We are returning to you the attached piece of correspondence which you mailed to our office. We are unable to process your request as submitted. We have kept no record of your submission." The next paragraph enumerated "the following six circumstances" under which the CPC-M provides client services in addition to "process[ing] Family Class Sponsorship applications where the Principal resides overseas." All the situations noted applied to my case and Kelie resides overseas. I was kind of very perplexed until I got to paragraph four which indicated that **"If you have not yet received correspondence from CPCM about your application**: Your sponsorship application is still waiting to be processed. Please retain the returned information and await further instructions from our office because we may determine that those items are not necessary for the sponsorship assessment portion. When we review your file, you may be instructed to send additional supporting documents to CPCM directly to facilitate the processing of your sponsorship application. Or you may be instructed to send those additional items directly to the visa office, to be attached to the APR [Application Processing Report?] which we have sent to the visa office for further processing." [Bold is original]

If I had been able to wait for this long to convince Kelie's mother on the need to have the child know her father is alive and always there for her, then a few months of waiting on the CIC was not going to be too much. I patiently waited, with the difficulty mostly being that of how to explain "why the repeated and lengthy process" to my daughter who has always been so keen on meeting her siblings and father on this side of the Atlantic. Finally, on November 22, 2012 the good news came with CIC's letter of that date to 'Dear Peter Ateh-Afac Fossungu':

This refers to the Application to Sponsor a Member of the Family Class you submitted to this office on behalf of Kelie Fossungu Tsopzem and family (if applicable)

You have met the Federal requirements for eligibility as a sponsor. Accordingly, the Application for Permanent Residence for your relative(s) has been forwarded to a visa office abroad for further processing.

Should you need to submit additional information or make any further enquiries regarding the Application for Permanent Residence for your relative(s), you may contact the visa office by e-mail, fax, or in writing as follows:

Embassy of Canada to Senegal in Dakar – Embassy of Canada, P.O. Box 3373, Dakar, Senegal. E-mail: Dakar@international.gc.ca. Fax number: 221-33-889-4720 [paragraphing altered here].

This visa office was selected based on your relative's home address and the requirements of the *Immigration and Refugee Protection Act*.

If you received this communication via email, please note that another copy will not be mailed to you.

I don't think I thought for a fleeting moment on reading this letter that I obviously received through my always active email (fossungupa@yahoo.ca) that there was another happier father than me in the whole wide world. At long last I was going to reunite with a child who has meant and caused so much to me. I immediately went to work to meet up with the "Provincial Requirements for Residents of Quebec" as directed in the above letter. After all the paper work and administrative procedures, Kelie's *Certificat de Sélection du Québec* (CSQ) was issued on January 15, 2013 and good till January 15, 2016. On February 21, 2013 I contacted the Embassy in Dakar inquiring about Application F000129083 as follows: "Dear Sir/Madam: I am writing just to make sure that you have not sent out communication to my daughter (Kelie Fossungu Tsopzem) and she has not yet received it. Thanks for your comprehension. Sincerely yours, Peter A. Fossungu [paragraphing altered]" On March 19, 2013 the Embassy's response was:

Dear applicant

In response to your email, we confirm that your file is pending review by an officer.

We currently [are] review[ing] files received in October 2011.Yours was received on 2012/05/02. Please visit the CIC website for more information on processing times of immigration   applications: @ http://www.cic.gc.ca/francais/information/delais/index.as p immigration. The delays indicated may vary depending on case complexity and volume of applications to process.

Rest assured that we are working to reduce processing times, and appreciate your patience.

You'll be receiving correspondence from Dakar visa's office as soon as the file is reviewed from the queue. For future reference, in all correspondence to our office, please refer to the applicant's full name, date of birth and file number.

Best regards

Service de l'Immigration | Immigration Section/NK
Annexe Ambassade du Canada | Embassy of Canada (Annex)
18, Rue Émile Zola Dakar, Sénégal
www.dakar.gc.ca
dakar.immigration@international.gc.ca

All was thus set and I was just joyfully waiting for the day I was to be informed by Kelie that her Landed Immigrant (Permanent Residence) documents have been received from Senegal for me to purchase her air ticket. But it looks like there are millions of persons out there who are just working to bring down all my efforts to make things better for the greatest number of persons possible. You can see that not only some of my family members would be found guilty of this tendency but that it is also done with the (in)active support of public agents in Canada. Thus, CIC would decide that poisoning my birthday is not enough pains for me and would go further to condemn my daughter for whatever offence they pin on her parents' mistake. I am talking about their unexpected letter of August 15, 2013 titled "THIS LETTER REPLACES THE ONE ISSUED ON SEPTEMBER 13, 2012" which ordained:

This refers to the Application to Sponsor a Member of the Family Class you submitted to this office on behalf of Kelie Fossungu Tsopzem and family (if applicable).

We have reviewed your application and regret to advise that you are not an eligible sponsor for the following reasons(s):

- You have not submitted an application for a member of the family class. You did not declare the applicant to Citizenship and Immigration Canada on your own Application for Permanent Residence or at the time you became permanent resident of Canada. As such, you do not meet regulation 117(9) (d). Please refer to the Immigration and Refugee Protection Regulation listed below for details.

You indicated on your sponsorship application that you wish to withdraw your application if found ineligible. As a result, your sponsorship application has been officially withdrawn and no further action will be taken. There is no right to appeal this decision.

A refund of all paid fees minus the sponsorship fee of $75 has been requested on your behalf. A cheque will be mailed to you at the above noted address in approximately six weeks

The Application for Permanent Residence for your relative(s) and all supporting documentation are hereby returned to you.

"There is no right to appeal this decision"! It is simply incredible that immigration officers could claim such powers to themselves in a country calling itself a democracy and with courts that are said to weld the power of judicial review of administrative and other acts. Is it really a *Hypocracy* or Democracy? Well, when I talk of "mechanical courts" in Canada you may have been thinking that only that institution is jammed with robots being regarded as human beings. Human beings obviously have feelings like Officer K. Would you want to regard Officer LLE (the architect of this outrageous replacing letter) as having any such human feelings, and not being a legalistic robot? Obviously, furthermore, isn't Officer LLE to the CPC-M as André Tremblay is to Revenue Quebec's Department of Pensions Alimentaires? Otherwise, why would he have chosen to very heartlessly go back almost a year later to rescind Officer K on the issue? Assuming that Officer K erred (which is far from the point), is it my daughter and I that have to bear the consequences of that error? And why must Officer LLE take that long to fix the so-called mistake of Officer K?

It cannot even be the issue of fixing a mistake. It is apparently one of behaving in a public office as if it is one's private property and thereby thinking that one is not to be questioned as to how that property is operated. I must point out that this CPC-M agent has a track record for all the negative responses on this file and would (like André Tremblay of Quebec) seem to be solely in total bad control of my file. Take all the CIC letters you have read above: January 19, 2011 (Officer DP), September 28, 2011 (Officer LLE), March 5, 2012 (Officer LLE), Undated (Case Processing Centre), November 22, 2012 (Officer K), and August 15, 2013 (Officer LLE). The maliciousness in Officer LLE's act can even be easily seen in the title of his vexatious letter: "THIS LETTER REPLACES THE ONE ISSUED ON SEPTEMBER 13, 2012". Yeah, Mr. Angry Public Servant! Try to keep your bitterness at home when you go to the office to serve, else it will rule you there completely rather than your reason ruling. I am telling you this because I have never received any letter from CIC dated September 13, 2012. Check the records. Officer K's letter that Officer LLE was so keen on nullifying is dated November 22, 2012 and NOT September 13, 2012. So, you would dare to argue that for close to a year the replacer could not master the exact date of what he was taking that long to cancel? It must be an erratic act, of course, you are saying? Otherwise, could Mr. Officer LLE of CPCM then kindly send me the letter he replaced on my 53rd birthday? Only the truth is consistent. And doesn't anyone think that I, of all the people in the world, needed the positive response, normally following on the heels of Officer K's letter, on that my Golden Plus Three Anniversary rather than Officer LLE's *tremblaybullshitation*?

The Third World War and the DNA Testing
Roundaboutism:

The road-blocking bullshit was not meant to terminate my efforts just there though. It was Officer LLE's long-term design to perpetuate our anguish. That is why I am actually hoping that some good people out there (and especially in CIC

126

itself) would valiantly come to my aid to make sure this innocent child (as all the others out there) should cease from endlessly suffering because of the evil or wrongful deeds of some adults that are entrusted with working toward the children's best interests. This CIC war is becoming tougher than I alone can correctly handle and any help would be enormously appreciated. I can be reached anytime by email preferably. I say it is becoming more and more difficult because of a number of reasons. First, my daughter has already become so weary of going through another fruitless process and prefers that I just be coming around often with her Canadian siblings to see her in Cameroon "since it is now clear that your Canada is not interested in seeing me come over there." Good suggestion from an overwhelmed child; but just how can that be achieved when: (1) I do not have the financial resources for making these intercontinental voyages (either alone or accompanied by the children) and (2) I don't have sole custody of any of her siblings here in Canada? The better option remains that of having Kelie come over to meet us but would *roundaboutism* let that happen one day?

Officer LLE's infamous 'replacing' letter enumerated 'Requirements for a New Sponsorship', indicating that "Should you wish to sponsor again, it will be necessary for you to: (1) submit a new sponsorship application with all required supporting documentation; (2) submit new processing fees; (3) meet all eligibility requirements for sponsorship; and (4) provide proof that the above-noted ineligibility has been resolved" (numbering supplied). Of course, there is no point in indicating that I wish to have my daughter here with me and her other siblings: even if it means fighting a tenth Immigration War (this book being a part of the Fourth). That is why I went into a third sponsorship in April 2014, making it more than clear in a "DNA BLOOD TESTING AS THE BASIS OF APPLICATION" letter dated April 17, 2014 (included in the Application) that "This letter is to notify you that this

Sponsorship Application in favour of my daughter, Kelie Fossungu Tsopzem, is to rely exclusively on DNA Blood Testing in proving whether or not we are father and daughter. Thank you. Sincerely, Peter Ateh-Afac Fossungu" (paragraphing altered). CIC received the application and sat on it, knowing well that there is just nothing we can do until they issue a request for the DNA testing. You get this *roundaboutist* strategy from earlier encounters.

On Wednesday, November 28, 2012 at 12.19 PM I sent Valery Stey an email titled "CIC Response," stating that "I wrote to CIC (letter here attached as KTF1) regarding the letter needed for the DNA testing but they have returned the correspondence with this letter (attached as KTF2 & 3) which is obviously not the letter you need. One of their agents also told me on the phone that such a letter from them was not necessary for you to carry the DNA testing. So I would like to know what the thing to do now is. Thanks. Peter." The same day Valery wrote back thanking me for my email and explained that:

DNA testing can be conducted, however because the CIC will not agree to it they now do not have to witness the sample collections and it makes it more difficult as it pertains to making the arrangements. This is now considered a private DNA test and not an immigration DNA test and there might be a chance that they may not accept the results if they suspect that witnessing of the samples overseas was not done in accordance.

So, short answer, is that you can do this test, but without any Embassy official witnessing it.

If you want to proceed, I would need to know where your daughter resides (I cannot recall from our past conversation).

Thanks.

Val

On Thursday, November 29, 2012 at 6.21 PM I therefore wrote thanking Valery for her speedy response and advice and indicating that "I think it is better I do not continue with the testing if CIC will not accept the results because the whole idea was for immigration purposes." On Thursday, January 10, 2013 at 12.52 PM Valery then wrote: "Hi Peter, I assume that there will not be any DNA testing proceeding? I will put in a request for a refund. There is a $100 + tax administrative fee for any cases that are closed per person collected (to cover costs for sample collection and courier). You paid a total of $371 (including taxes) and a refund of $222.68 + taxes will be refunded. Please confirm your current mailing address in full so that a cheque can be sent to you. Many thanks, Val" (paragraphing altered). The next day at 12.31 AM I confirmed the address to be 7225 Rue De Nancy #325, Montreal, Quebec H3R 2L8 at which I later got the refund.

As you can then see, Officer LLE had long determined that there was no way whatever that Kelie would ever come to Canada, with his decision being not appealable! What is the use of having DNA Testing as a means of proving paternity (for instance) in CIC's requirements when that means would be unavailable to certain persons? I ask this particular question because my third April 17, 2014 Sponsorship Application clearly made it clear the whole thing was based on DNA Testing, as per this letter of same date included in the application package that has been outlined already. Thus, the only acknowledgement of the receipt of the April 2014 Application was just a letter demanding its completion with a new signed form.[62] Thereafter, there was a repetition of

---

[62] I received this letter by email on June 9, 2014 and it indicated that
Your application is incomplete: you will find details of the item(s) that are missing from this application below:
• You must provide a current and completed Application to Sponsor, Sponsorship Agreement and Undertaking (IMM 1344) bearing

Officer LLE's replacing letter, with the sole difference just being that it is dated on October 30, 2014 and instead signed by Officer NGR:

Dear PETER ATEH AFAC FOSSUNGU: This refers to the Application to Sponsor a Member of the Family Class you submitted to this office on behalf of KELIE FOSSUNGU TSOPZEM and family (if applicable). We have reviewed your application and regret to advise that you are not an eligible sponsor for the following reason(s): You have not submitted an application for a member of the family class. You did not declare the applicant to Citizenship and Immigration Canada on your own Application for Permanent Residence or at the time you became permanent resident of Canada. As such, you do not meet regulation 117(9Xd). Please refer to the Immigration and Refugee Protection Regulations listed below for details. You indicated on your sponsorship application that you wish to withdraw your application if found ineligible. As a result, your sponsorship application has been officially withdrawn and no further action will be taken. There is no right to appeal this decision. A refund of all paid fees minus the sponsorship fee of $75 has been requested on your behalf. A cheque will be mailed to you at the above noted address in approximately six weeks. The Application for Permanent Residence for your relative(s) and all supporting documentation are hereby returned to you. Requirements for a New Sponsorship Should you wish to sponsor again, it will be

---

signatures. This form is available at http://www.cic.gc.ca/english/information/application/fc.asp.

All requested documents/information and a copy of this letter must be resubmitted within 45 days of the date of this letter in order to be processed. If you are unable to provide any of the requested documents/information, please explain why they are not available.

If the information/documents requested have not been submitted within the timeframe listed above, your entire unprocessed application will be returned to you. (underlining is original)

I sent the required information/documents immediately.

130

necessary for you to: submit a new sponsorship application with all required supporting documentation; submit new processing fees; meet all eligibility requirements for sponsorship; and provide proof that the above-noted ineligibility has been resolved.... (Paragraphing altered)

Yes, of course. Just keep on wasting your time applying, that is what it boils down to.

Conclusion

The entire show here must surely remind any sensible person that Canadian institutions may have so many things in mind, with the best interest of children not being among them; or, if it figures at all, it is at the very bottom of the lengthy list of their economic and business priorities. From the demonstrations drawn from my rich and agonizing *expibasketism* I am sure you can be able to teach much about, promote, and to portray Canada as it has never been properly understood, not only by outsiders but also by Canadians themselves. This book has therefore made extensive and detailed use of that *expibasketism* to deliver the message that Canada is not at all the 'children's-best-interests-friendly' nation that it is often mistaken for. Canada may be what it claims to be but, since a country or community can only be correctly seen through the workings of the institutions that incarnate it, this study on Canadian institutions and children's best interests has dared to show a contrary portrait. Its documentations and proofs point to the unsavoury conclusion that most of the institutions that are supposedly there to carter for and protect children and promote their wellbeing and glowing future often end up in reality instead actively working against said children and all what their best interest should properly signify. A child's best interest, in my humble opinion, certainly does not necessarily entail the worst interest of one of its parents; making it very hard to see why a parent who relentlessly works towards frustrating a partner's advances has their children's best interest in mind.

If Flavie thinks she can unnecessarily hang on these children in order to use them to fix her broken immigration issues, I have got news for her. The sane way these children were to aid in the regularization of her situation in Canada was through the Sponsorships that she wantonly blew up because of her propensity to heed only to uninformed counsel from outside her matrimonial home. Having children in Canada alone is just not enough to fix a refugee claimant's case that has gone wrong. Neither would the church now come in to savage it. There are several cases to cite here but I would like to stay within the Cameroonian community here in Montreal and proffer the *Fuh-Cham* case.

According to Roger Ekuh-Ngwese's report, the Cameroon Diaspora in Montreal and a local Catholic Church in LaSalle had a face-off with the Canadian Immigration Minister and the House of Commons after an Immigration Judge handed down his verdict on one of the hundreds of asylum cases in a Montreal Court. Hilary Fuh-Cham, Yvette Fuh-Cham and their three kids, two of whom were born in Canada were at the brink of deportation to Cameroon following the Judge's decision. The Fuh-Chams therefore turned to their local Catholic congregation (St. John Brebeauf Church) and the LaSalle community for strength and support, commencing the process of gathering sufficient signatures towards submission of a petition to pressure the government to reconsider the deportation verdict.[63] Both parents were active in the community and working and contributing to the Quebec and Canadian economies (unlike Flavie) but all those steps taken never changed the IRB decision and the family was still deported to Cameroon in late 2014.

---

[63] See Rekngwese, "Family battle deportation to Cameroon" (posted on September 16, 2014)

@ http://www.diasporatalk.com/family-battle-deportation-to-cameroon/

References

Asahchop v. Fossungu – *Scholastica Achankeng Asahchop v Peter Ateh-Afac Fossungu*, London Family High Court, File N° 1162-05.

Dwomoh, Richard (2010) *The UN Security Council and Small Arms Proliferation: Legislating the Illicit Trade in Arms* (Lambert Academic Publishing).

Fossungu v. Bayiha – *Peter Ateh-Afac Fossungu v. Henriette-Flavi Bayiha*, Suit N° 500-04-060196-137 of Montreal's Cour Supérieure, Chambre de la Famille.

Fossungu, Peter Ateh-Afac (2015a) *Africans and Negative Competition in Canadian Factories: Revamping Canada's Immigration, Employment and Welfare Policies?* (Bamenda: Langaa RPCIG).

_____ (2015b) *Family Politics and Deception in Northern North America and West-Central Africa: Litigating God's Marriage Intention?* (Bamenda: Langaa RPCIG).

_____ (2015c) *The HISOFE Dictionary of Midnight Politics: Expibasketical Theories on Afrikentication and African Unity* (Bamenda: Langaa RPCIG).

_____ (2014) *Africa's Anthropological Dictionary on Love and Understanding: Marriage and the Tensions of Belonging in Cameroon* (Bamenda, Cameroon: Langaa RPCIG).

_____ (2013) *Africans in Canada: Blending Canadian and African Lifestyles?* (Bamenda, Cameroon: Langaa RPCIG).

Ngwafor, Ephraim N. (No Year) *Ngwafor's Law Students Examination Guide: Family Law* (Limbe: Jotan Printers).

Rekngwese, "Family battle deportation to Cameroon" (posted on September 16, 2014) @ http://www.diasporatalk.com/family-battle-deportation-to-cameroon/